QUESTIONS & ANSWERS:
ANTITRUST

QUESTIONS & ANSWERS:
ANTITRUST

Multiple-Choice and Short-Answer Questions and Answers

Shubha Ghosh
Vilas Research Fellow & Professor of Law, and
Associate Director, INSITE
University of Wisconsin Law School

ISBN: 978-0-7698-5421-2 (print)

ISBN: 978-0-3271-7973-3 (eBook)

> NOTE TO USERS
> To ensure that you are using the latest materials available in this area, please be sure to periodically check the LexisNexis Law School web site for downloadable updates and supplements at www.lexisnexis.com/lawschool.

Editorial Offices
121 Chanlon Rd., New Providence, NJ 07974 (908) 464-6800
201 Mission St., San Francisco, CA 94105-1831 (415) 908-3200
www.lexisnexis.com

MATTHEW◆BENDER

ABOUT THE AUTHOR

Shubha Ghosh is Vilas Research Fellow and Professor of Law at University of Wisconsin Law School. He teaches and writes in the areas of intellectual property law and competition policy. He earned his bachelor's degree from Amherst College, his doctoral degree in economics from The University of Michigan, and his JD from Stanford.

PREFACE

Antitrust law offers many challenges to students and practitioners. Antitrust opinions are fact intensive, filled with legal analysis informed by economic policy analysis and business history. Cases can be long and difficult to read, and the legal arguments, technical. In many ways, the study and practice of antitrust law brings together the various tools of legal analysis you might encounter in law school: common law thinking, statutory interpretation, constitutional analysis, administrative law, and international law.

The challenges of Antitrust law is what makes the course an exciting one. If you are interested in intellectual property, economic regulation, business policy, or legal history, the study of Antitrust law will be rewarding. A study guide like this one provides a review and test of the knowledge you have gleaned from your course. Although the problems in this book are not keyed to any one of the many Antitrust law casebooks on the market, the questions are structured around the major antitrust cases, antitrust history, and antitrust statutory provisions that all casebooks and courses cover. Working through the following questions will give you a valuable review and preparation for your course's final exam.

Each student will find different ways to review these questions. One way is to review the questions after you finish one of the topics covered by a specific chapter. The Index and the Table of Contents provide key terms to guide you through the questions and connect them to materials covered in your Antitrust course. The Answers offer detailed discussion of the doctrines being tested in the Questions and include citations to relevant cases and statutes. Not only can the Questions and Answers test your knowledge, they can be helpful in developing your outline for the course.

What I hope you learn beyond the rules of Antitrust law is the challenge of Antirust law and policy. Once you get beyond the challenges, you will find Antitrust law engaging and intellectually rewarding. Enjoy!

Shubha Ghosh
Madison, WI

TABLE OF CONTENTS

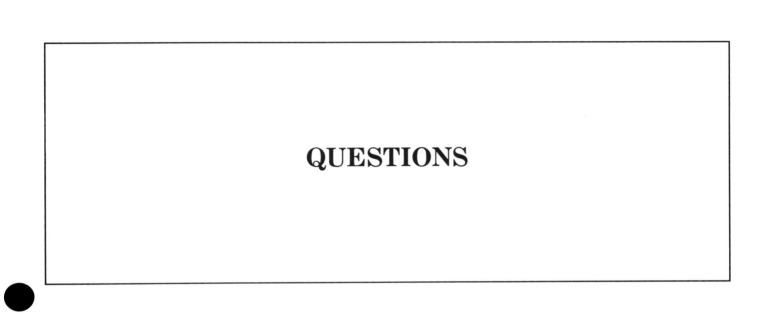

QUESTIONS

1. The Sherman Act

    (A) is the first body of law in the United States to deal with competition and regulation of markets.

    (B) has its roots in the English common law on restraint of trade.

    (C) creates a civil remedy for monopolization, but no criminal penalties.

    (D) has as its primary goal the maximization of wealth.

2. Which of these statements is an accurate one about antitrust policy?

    (A) Antitrust policy is guided exclusively by the goal of ensuring markets consists of small firms that support start-ups of new businesses.

    (B) Antitrust policy is guided by goals of economic efficiency primarily with minimal concerns for access to markets by small firms.

    (C) Antitrust policy is concerned with static and short term gains and focuses less on the dynamics of the market.

    (D) Antitrust policy aids in ensuring markets work effectively and efficiently to reach goals of wealth maximization and distribution of market gains among consumers and firms.

3. During the first twenty years of the Sherman Act:

    (A) Courts had little discretion in determining antitrust laws and policies.

    (B) The Department of Justice brought no antitrust suits based on violation of the antitrust laws.

    (C) Courts sometimes interpreted the Sherman Act literally striking down any agreement among competitors whether or not the agreement was reasonable.

    (D) Monopolization was considered legal if acquired through skill or good fortune.

4. Congress' goal in enacting the Sherman Act was to

    (A) codify what was believed to be the English common law on restraint of trade.

(B) abrogate the common law on restraint of trade in favor of statutory law.

(C) adopt the British statutes on antitrust law to the United States context.

(D) protect large companies that had organized into trusts as a way of doing business.

5. Under the English common law on restraint of trade,

(A) a covenant not to compete was always per se illegal.

(B) a covenant not to compete was sometimes permitted in the case of a sale of a business.

(C) a covenant not to compete was illegal as an ancillary restraint.

(D) a covenant not to compete was always reasonable unless the covenant was used in the dissolution of a partnership.

6. An ancillary restraint

(A) was per se illegal under the English common law.

(B) is a restraint secondary to a primary agreement.

(C) was legal under the English common law, but per se illegal under the Sherman Act.

(D) was recognized under the Sherman Act as sometimes illegal.

7. Economic efficiency

(A) is the sole policy goal of antitrust law.

(B) means that all resources are used to maximize surplus to consumers and producers.

(C) occurs through exchange between a seller and a buyer.

(D) is ensured through preventing agreements in restraint of trade.

8. Which of the following is the most accurate statement?

(A) Monopolization occurs through several firms agreeing to set price.

(B) Antitrust law deals solely with agreements among sellers, but not buyers.

(C) Section One of the Sherman Act makes illegal agreements between two or more firms while Section Two makes illegal anticompetitive conduct by one firm.

(D) The Sherman Act has as its primary goal the breaking up of large companies into smaller ones that can agree on how to promote the marketplace.

9. In the early years, the Sherman Act

(A) regulated only business entities, but did not interfere with conduct by labor unions.

(B) was used by the Department of Justice to make intellectual property licenses illegal as forms of monopolization.

(C) was interpreted the courts to make restraints on trade illegal even if arguably reasonable.

(D) tracked the English common law on restraint of trade except for its treatment of partnerships.

10. Which of the following statements is the least accurate?

(A) In the early years of the Sherman Act, interpretation of the law was left largely to the courts with the agencies taking on more importance over time.

(B) The Department of Justice and the Federal Trade Commission have different powers under the antitrust laws and disagree on the treatment of mergers and acquisitions.

(C) The Federal Trade Commission's jurisdiction is pursuant to the Federal Trade Commission Act which deals with unfair or deceptive business practices.

(D) The Department of Justice has broad sub poena powers to aid in its criminal investigations of antitrust violations.

SHORT ANSWER QUESTIONS: Please write a one paragraph response of about five to ten sentences to each of the following.

11. What are some of the policies underlying U.S. antitrust laws?

ANSWER:

12. Antitrust laws in the United States are enforced privately or through state agencies. Briefly compare and contrast the two means of enforcement.

ANSWER:

13. Which of the following is the most accurate statement about a perfectly competitive market?

    (A) Firms own intellectual property that serve to limit ease of entry into the market.

    (B) Firms take the market price as given as do consumers

    (C) Firms earn above normal profits in the long run since competition promotes returns to investment.

    (D) Each consumer pays a different price for the product or service based on willingness to pay.

14. A monopoly is a market in which

    (A) there are a few firms who engage in strategic behavior in price setting.

    (B) a single firm sets price and quantity in order to prevent other firms from entering.

    (C) a single firm sets price based on the market demand in order to maximize profit.

    (D) a single firm integrates with all other firms to prevent new entrants.

15. Which of the following is the least accurate statement about an oligopoly market?

    (A) An oligopoly market has low barriers to entry so that many firms can enter in the long run.

    (B) Firms in an oligopoly market can collude to prevent new firms from entering.

    (C) Firms in an oligopoly market can compete over price and other attributes of a product or service.

    (D) An oligopoly market exhibits dead weight loss and excess capacity.

16. Own price elasticity of demand (also known as price elasticity of demand or elasticity of demand):

    (A) measures how quantity demanded in a marketplace changes when price and income change.

(B) measures how quantity demanded in a marketplace changes when a new product is introduced in a marketplace.

(C) measures how quantity demanded in a marketplace changes when new consumers enter into a marketplace.

(D) measure how quantity demanded in a marketplace changes when the price for the product or service changes.

17. Which of the following is true of own price elasticity of demand?

(A) The closer own price elasticity is to zero, the more inelastic is market demand with respect to price.

(B) The availability of substitute products or services that consumers can switch to if the price rises will make market demand more elastic with respect to price.

(C) Neither A nor B.

(D) Both A and B.

18. Elasticity of supply depends upon

(A) the ease with which consumers can substitute to other products or service.

(B) the ease with which new firms can enter when there is a price change in the marketplace.

(C) the ease with which new technologies spread among existing firms.

(D) the ease with which a firm can raise the market price.

19. The Lerner Index

(A) is a measure of market concentration based solely on market share.

(B) is a measure of market concentration based on the number of firms in a market or industry.

(C) is a measure of market concentration based on the own price elasticity of demand, elasticity of supply, and market share.

(D) is equal to zero if a market is a monopoly.

20. A profit maximizing monopolist will

(A) charge a price equal to the marginal cost of production.

(B) charge a price on the market demand curve where demand is relatively inelastic.

(C) charge a price that is a markup of marginal cost where the markup is based on elasticity of demand.

(D) charge a price in order to ensure that competitors leave the market.

21. Market power measures

(A) a firm's ability to deter entry.

(B) a firm's ability to affect the market price.

(C) a firm's ability to affect market quantity.

(D) All of the above.

22. Which of the following is the most accurate statement about using market share as a measure of market power?

(A) A high market share means that a firm has market power, and a low market share means that a firm has no market power.

(B) A high market share combined with a low elasticity of demand and low elasticity of supply would suggest the existence of market power.

(C) A low market share can indicate market power if elasticity of demand is also low.

(D) A low market share supports a conclusion that a firm lacks market power.

23. The Lerner Index as a measure of market power

(A) is a reliable measure since a firm with market power will price above marginal cost.

(B) is flawed because the index assumes that we know what the relevant market is.

(C) is a reliable measure as long as current market conditions are stable and not changing.

(D) is flawed because the numbers can be manipulated by firms in the market.

24. Which of the following is the least accurate statement about market definition?

(A) Cross price elasticity can be used to determine which goods or services should be classified as in the same market as long as one is aware of the elasticity's limitations.

(B) Cross price elasticity is flawed because a high cross price elasticity is consistent with above cost pricing in a given market.

(C) Cross price elasticity as a tool for market definition can result in misidentifying a monopolized market as competitive.

(D) Cross price elasticity measures the degree to which two goods or services are substitutes and therefore a high cross price of elasticity would imply that the two goods or services are in separate markets.

25. Which of the following factors should be among those taken into account in market definition?

   (A) Geography, time, cross price elasticities.

   (B) Market share, Lerner Index, and price markups.

   (C) Elasticities of demand and supply, market Share.

   (D) Elasticity of supply, number of firms, market share.

26. A price cartel

   (A) is stable in a monopoly market.

   (B) is unstable since new firms can always enter.

   (C) is stable if firms in the cartel can monitor and punish each other.

   (D) is unstable since firms can see when one firm in the cartel undercuts another.

27. Which of the following statements is the most accurate about price discrimination?

   (A) Price discrimination serves as a way for firms in a perfectly competitive market to differentiate their product.

   (B) Price discrimination can result in improving market efficiency by allowing some consumers to have access to a product that they otherwise would not if a firm had to charge a single price.

   (C) Price discrimination allows a firm to charge a higher price to a consumer with a lower willingness to pay and a lower price to a consumer willing to pay more.

   (D) Price discrimination always results in consumers in a market being worse off since the price discriminating firm will always obtain the consumer surplus.

SHORT ANSWER QUESTIONS: Please write a one paragraph response of about five to ten sentences to each of the following.

28. Explain how economic theory informs the view of competition in U.S. antitrust law.
ANSWER:

29. Explain how the concept of elasticity is used in U.S. antitrust law.
ANSWER:

30. A private right of action under Section 4 of the Clayton Act

    (A) can be brought by any purchaser of a product sold in a market where there has been anticompetitive conduct.

    (B) requires injury to person or property.

    (C) is available only for treble damages, but not for injunctions.

    (D) can result in treble damages to compensate for any injury either economic or non-economic.

31. Which of the following would be an example of an antitrust injury?

    (A) A firm facing increased competition and loss in profits because a competing firm that was about to go out of business was acquired by another firm.

    (B) A gas merchant loses profits because of an agreement between a manufacturer and another gas merchant to set the maximum retail price for gasoline.

    (C) A union sues an association for urging parties not to do business with union firms.

    (D) A purchaser buys a product directly from a firm that has engaged in a price fixing scheme with competitors.

32. An indirect purchaser of a product has standing to sue

    (A) when the purchaser buys from an intermediary in a vertical situation who is a nonconspirator.

    (B) when the purchaser buys from a retailer who has entered into a vertical price fixing agreement with the manufacturer.

    (C) when the purchaser is seeking damages but not when seeking an injunction.

    (D) when the purchaser entered into a pre-existing, fixed quantity, cost-plus contract with the first purchaser who can pass on the overcharge at his discretion.

33. Plaintiff alleges a conspiracy occurring outside the United States in an antitrust action brought in a federal court in United States. Which of the following is the least accurate?

    (A) A Clayton Act claim would be dismissed for lack of jurisdiction.

(B) A Sherman Act claim would not be dismissed if the conspiracy had an effect on commerce in the United States and there is no conflict with foreign law or policy.

(C) Both Clayton Act and Sherman Act claims would survive.

(D) The Sherman Act claim would be dismissed if the allegations did not give the court subject matter jurisdiction.

34. Under the Noerr-Pennington doctrine,

(A) all economic boycotts implemented to influence the passage of legislation is subject to review under the antitrust laws.

(B) lobbying and other legislative efforts to influence the laws are immune from antitrust review even if they have an anticompetitive effect unless such efforts are a sham.

(C) lobbying is not immune from antitrust review if the lobbying results in legislation that hurts a competitor.

(D) governmental action such as an administrative proceeding is always immune from antitrust review.

35. A natural monopoly

(A) is immune from the antitrust laws.

(B) may be subject to regulation, which might be the basis for antitrust immunity.

(C) need not be regulated because markets are contestable.

(D) will be liable for treble damages if it tries to raise prices.

36. Suppose Congress creates an agency to regulate the market for software. When would the existence of such regulatory agency immunize firms in the software industry from antitrust review?

(A) The agency has jurisdiction over the challenged practice, and the antitrust laws would interfere with the regulation.

(B) The regulation is so pervasive that Congress is assumed to determined that competition is inadequate in vindicating the public interest.

(C) The pertinent statute or regulations has an express provision that states antitrust law should not apply.

(D) All of the above.

37. Which of the following is exempted from the antitrust laws?

(A) Union activity to determine and control wages.

  (B) A firm engaged in the business of insurance.

  (C) Export association whose activities have a direct and substantial effect on U.S. commerce.

  (D) A family farm.

38. California passes a statute that restricts entry into the market for wine. Such a statute

  (A) would make the state and the wineries liable under the antitrust laws.

  (B) would make the wineries but not the state liable under the antitrust laws.

  (C) would not be a basis for liability of California under the state action doctrine.

  (D) would immunize California only if the courts compelled the state to pass the legislation and the courts supervise the implementation of the legislation.

39. A municipal zoning board is put in charge of restricting the entry of new bars into town. The zoning board

  (A) is immune from antitrust scrutiny under the state action doctrine.

  (B) is liable for violations of the antitrust law because its restriction on entry of new firms is a restraint of trade.

  (C) is immune if the program to restrict entry is compelled by the state which also actively supervises the board.

  (D) is liable for violations if the restriction on entry tends to monopolize the market for bars in the municipality.

40. A Civil Investigative Demand (CID)

  (A) gives private parties broad powers to subpoena witnesses in an antitrust case.

  (B) is a tool used by the Department of Justice to subpoena witnesses in a criminal investigation of antitrust violations.

  (C) is used by the Federal Trade Commission exclusively to subpoena witnesses.

  (D) can be used by private parties only upon authorization from the Department of Justice.

41. Section 7 of the Clayton Act

  (A) governs review of mergers and acquisitions.

  (B) allows only private parties to bring suit to challenge a merger or acquisition.

(C) allows the DoJ or FTC to challenge a merger or acquisition as having adverse effects on competition.

(D) allows the FTC alone to challenge a merger or acquisition.

42. A firm sues a competitor for a breach of contract. The firm's goal is to disrupt the competitor's business and possibly make the competitor bankrupt. Which of the following is the most accurate about these facts?

(A) The firm is liable for an antitrust violation.

(B) The firm is immune from antitrust liability.

(C) The firm is immune unless the lawsuit is both objectively and subjectively baseless.

(D) The firm is immune because it is engaging in state action.

43. The attorney general of a state can bring a suit under the federal antitrust laws

(A) always.

(B) only if there is a corresponding state antitrust law, also known as a Baby Sherman Act.

(C) only if the Department of Justice decides not to bring suit.

(D) if the state has standing to sue and there is antitrust injury.

44. The Federal Government through its agencies

(A) is immune from the antitrust laws.

(B) in general is not immune from the antitrust laws, but antitrust enforcement cannot conflict with other federal policy.

(C) is liable if the Department of Justice brings a false antitrust claim.

(D) is immune for actions for treble damages, but not injunctions.

SHORT ANSWER QUESTIONS: Please write a one paragraph response of about five to ten sentences to each of the following.

45. Explain the concept of antitrust immunity and the State Action Doctrine.

ANSWER:

46. Explain the Noerr-Pennington Doctrine and the policy reason for the immunity.

ANSWER:

47. Which of the following is a true statement about the rule of reason analysis under Section One of the Sherman Act?

   (A) The rule of reason applies to all vertical restraints while per se analysis applies to all horizontal ones.

   (B) Territorial restrictions are subject to the rule of reason.

   (C) Rule of reason entails a comparison of anticompetitive effects of a restraint with its procompetitive justifications.

   (D) Per se analysis applies to all restraints under the language of the Sherman Act.

48. Per se analysis means

   (A) that an agreement is illegal if it has harmful effects.

   (B) that an agreement is illegal on its face even if there is no market power.

   (C) that an agreement is illegal only if there is market power.

   (D) that an agreement is illegal if the presumption of illegality cannot be rebutted.

49. The quick look rule of reason

   (A) means that an agreement is presumed to be illegal unless there is a procompetitive justification.

   (B) means that an agreement will be upheld under a presumption of legality.

   (C) means that an agreement is per se illegal unless there is no market power.

   (D) means that a court will review an agreement with little scrutiny and under a lower standard of review than a full rule of reason analysis.

50. Price fixing is per se illegal

   (A) only if there are anticompetitive effects that outweigh procompetitive benefits.

   (B) because dividing the market among competitors could lead to monopolization.

   (C) even if there is no market power.

(D) only if prices are raised above marginal cost for more than a transitory period of time.

51. A cartel is likely to be strong if

(A) more than half of the firms in the cartel have market power.

(B) firms can monitor each other to ensure there is no cheating through expansions in quantity or price cutting.

(C) the product sold is heterogeneous and difficult to measure.

(D) the number of firms in the cartel covers the entire market.

52. Because firms in an industry are concerned with the quality of the product that they sell, they decide to restrict how much each firm produces and distributes in the marketplace. The firms agree that such restrictions will help to improve the quality of the product. Which of the following statements is an accurate assessment of these facts?

(A) Since the firms do not agree to a price, the agreement is subject to the rule of reason.

(B) The agreement is per se legal because of the pro-consumer justification in improving quality.

(C) The agreement is per se illegal because the anticompetitive effects are not rebutted by a procompetitive justification.

(D) The agreement is per se illegal because output restrictions operate like price setting agreements.

53. Under the ancillary restraint doctrine,

(A) a restraint is illegal only if it fails the rule of reason.

(B) a restraint is always per se illegal.

(C) a restraint that is ancillary to an agreement is illegal only if it is unreasonable.

(D) a restraint that is ancillary to an agreement is illegal only if there is market power.

54. The quick look rule of reason applies

(A) if the anticompetitive effects of an agreement are intuitively obvious.

(B) only when firms have market power.

(C) only when the agreement deals with price.

(D) in cases involving professional associations.

55. A professional association agrees that in order to promote quality and respect for the profession, members of the association cannot compete with each other. Such an agreement

   (A) is illegal only if the antitrust plaintiff can show harm to the market resulting from the agreement.

   (B) is legal since professional associations are held to a lower standard under the antitrust laws.

   (C) is illegal since competition is more likely to improve quality and respect for the profession.

   (D) is legal since improving the profession is a business justification.

56. Price fixing may be found reasonable

   (A) if there is no market power.

   (B) if an industry is in crisis and higher prices might improve market conditions for supply.

   (C) if the government approves the agreement through joint DOJ and FTC review.

   (D) if the firms agree to raise prices jointly only for a short period of time.

57. An agreement among members of a professional association is

   (A) per se legal.

   (B) illegal only if there are anticompetitive effects.

   (C) will likely be per se illegal if the agreement is to directly control price and there is no public interest justification.

   (D) legal only if there is a business justification.

58. Private law schools as part of their university accreditation process must disclose information about tuition and other costs. This disclosure of information among firms in an industry

   (A) is per se legal.

   (B) is likely to be found legal if the information includes only past data, generally aggregated, and does not support an agreement to set price.

   (C) is likely to be found illegal if the parties to the agreement have market power collectively.

   (D) is per se illegal because any sharing of price information can be used to set price in the market.

59. Firm A agrees with Firm B to never enter into Firm B's territory if Firm B also agrees to not enter Firm A's territory. This agreement

    (A) is illegal if the two firms have market power.

    (B) is per se illegal even if the firms do not agree to price or to output and even if the two firms never competed with each other.

    (C) is legal if the agreement has no effect on price or output in the marketplace.

    (D) is legal if the two firms lack market power.

60. Market power under Section One

    (A) is never relevant.

    (B) is irrelevant when reviewing a price fixing agreement but may be relevant for an agreement with a strong business justification.

    (C) may be relevant in assessing the legality of an agreement under the rule of reason.

    (D) is relevant if a firm is attempting to monopolize a market.

61. An agreement among competitors to set a maximum price

    (A) is treated the same under Section One as an agreement to set a minimum price.

    (B) can be understood as being analyzed under a quick look rule of reason.

    (C) is per se legal.

    (D) is illegal only if the agreement is part of one to divide territories among competitors.

62. Joint ventures among firms to engage in research and development or in product distribution

    (A) are per se legal because of the strong business justification.

    (B) have been analyzed under the rule of reason because joint ventures yield economic efficiencies.

    (C) have been considered per se illegal because of the effect on price in the marketplace.

    (D) are not per se illegal if they engage in price setting since a joint venture is considered one entity and not two.

63. Under the National Cooperative Research Act of 1984 (amended in 1993),

    (A) all joint ventures are subject to the rule of reason.

(B) joint ventures that deal with research and development must register and can qualify for rule of reason treatment.

(C) joint ventures that are found to be in violation of the Sherman Act can be subject to treble damages.

(D) joint ventures are subject to a quick look rule of reason.

64. A group boycott

(A) is an agreement among competitors to not deal with a specific supplier, customer, or other competitor.

(B) can be subject to either a per se or rule of reason treatment depending on the circumstances.

(C) is a type of concerted refusal to deal.

(D) All of the above.

65. A concerted refusal to deal

(A) will be subject to a rule of reason if a professional association forms the agreement.

(B) will be subject to per se treatment if the refusal to deal is supporting a price fixing or other per se illegal agreement.

(C) will be legal if there is a strong business justification based on creating market efficiencies.

(D) will be subject to rule of reason if the agreement is among direct competitors.

66. Market divisions among competitors

(A) can occur through territorial divisions, product divisions, or customer divisions.

(B) are often found to be legal because of the business justification of preventing free riding by one competitor of another competitor's investment in providing customer services and promoting quality.

(C) are legal if the agreement to divide markets does not also include an agreement on price.

(D) are per se illegal unless there is a business justification.

67. To establish liability for price fixing,

(A) the antitrust plaintiff must show an express agreement to raise prices.

(B) the antitrust plaintiff must show a contract or conspiracy, either express or implied.

(C) the antitrust plaintiff must show market power.

(D) the antitrust plaintiff must show an anticompetitive effect.

68. Which of the following set of factors are part of the "plus factors" to show conscious parallelism?

(A) Defendants engaged in a radical departure from prior practice, had an express agreement, and actually participated in the scheme.

(B) Defendants were aware of solicitation of co-defendants to participate in scheme, had market power, and engaged in interdependent action.

(C) Defendants had a substantial profit motive to engage in the scheme, actually participated in the scheme, and engaged in a radical departure from prior practice.

(D) Defendants expressly agreed to a per se illegal act, had a substantial profit motive, and engaged in a radical departure from prior practice.

69. With regards to conscious parallelism, the Department of Justice has taken the view that

(A) a noncompetitive price structure and little likelihood of independent action are preconditions for use of facilitating devices by oligopolists.

(B) parallel conduct is one factor to look for in detecting an implicit agreement to fix prices in an oligopoly.

(C) All of the above.

(D) None of the above.

70. Which of the following is an example of two firms engaging in a contract or conspiracy in violation of the Sherman Act?

(A) A corporation and its wholly owned subsidiary agreeing to set price.

(B) Two oil companies forming a joint venture to engage in oil refining which sets the price charged to distributors.

(C) A trade association agreement to fix prices charged by its members.

(D) Agents of a corporation making decisions binding the corporation in the marketplace.

71. One difference between criminal and civil enforcement under the Sherman Act is

(A) specific intent must be shown for criminal liability.

(B) anticompetitive effects must be shown for criminal liability while civil liability can be based on a per se rule.

(C) general recklessness can be basis for criminal liability.

(D) either specific or general intent can be shown for criminal liability with anticompetitive effects serving as evidence of general intent.

SHORT ANSWER QUESTIONS: Please write a one paragraph response of about five to ten sentences to each of the following.

72. What is a horizontal agreement?

ANSWER:

73. What are the differences between a per se rule and the rule of reason?

ANSWER:

74. Which of the following is the least accurate statement about the difference between vertical and horizontal restraints?

   (A) A vertical restraint is among parties in various parts of the distribution chain while a horizontal restraint is among direct competitors.

   (B) Vertical restraints are subject to rule of reason while horizontal restraints are subject to a per se rule.

   (C) Vertical restraints are enforced under the Sherman Act and the Clayton Act while horizontal restraints are enforced mainly under the Sherman Act.

   (D) Vertical restraints, like horizontal restraints, may sometimes enhance efficiency and competition.

75. The economic effect of a vertical price restraint, either maximum or minimum,

   (A) is to reduce economic efficiency by reducing competition.

   (B) may increase efficiency by allowing better provision of services but may have an ambiguous effect on consumer welfare.

   (C) reduces consumer welfare by preventing a retailer from cutting price below a minimum floor set by the manufacturer.

   (D) increases consumer welfare by allowing consumers to obtain better services from a retailer.

76. A vertical non-price restraint

   (A) allows retailers to enter into a market more effectively by lowering prices.

   (B) increases economic efficiency by allowing prices to fluctuate according to supply and demand.

   (C) allows manufacturers to restrict retailers in a certain region and thereby limit free riding in the provision of services and limit intrabrand competition.

   (D) requires retailers to obtain all their requirements from a single manufacturer.

77. Horizontal restraints on price

(A) generally reduces price competition that benefits consumers.

(B) eliminates intrabrand competition.

(C) allows firms to more effectively invest in services.

(D) benefits consumers by allowing firms to provide better quality products and services.

78. A dual distributorship

(A) arises when a manufacturer sells products to consumers both directly and through retailers.

(B) is per se illegal.

(C) is per se legal.

(D) arises when there is a cartel among retailers to force manufacturers to impose minimum resale price maintenance.

79. Which of the following is a true statement about vertical restraints?

(A) The antitrust treatment of price restraints evolved from a rule of reason to per se rules.

(B) Both price and non-price restraints are analyzed under the rule of reason.

(C) Maximum resale price maintenance is subject to the per se rule unless accompanied by a non-price restraint.

(D) Maximum resale price maintenance is a disguised form of minimum resale price maintenance.

80. Minimum resale price maintenance

(A) was per se illegal unless established as part of a consignment agreement.

(B) was always subject to the rule of reason unless the harm to consumers was obvious.

(C) was per se illegal when enacted by a patent owner.

(D) was subject to the rule of reason when required by the retailer rather than the manufacturer.

81. Which of the following is a false statement about vertical non-price restraints?

(A) A restriction that only authorized retailers can sell a product is an example of a vertical non-price restraint.

(B) The Supreme Court for a brief period of time treated vertical non-price restraints as per se illegal.

(C) The Supreme Court shifted the standard for vertical non-price restraints from per se to rule of reason in response to changes in the law on the treatment of minimum resale price maintenance.

(D) Vertical non-price restraints can enhance efficiency by reducing intrabrand competition and thereby increase interbrand competition.

82. If a manufacturer imposes a vertical non-price restraint to limit the number of retailers in a geographic area,

(A) then imposing minimum resale prices serves to prevent potential exercise of market power by retailers.

(B) then imposing maximum resale prices serves to allow retailers to invest more intensively in services and prevent cost cutting.

(C) then imposing minimum resale prices serves to prevent the entry of new firms.

(D) then imposing maximum resale prices serves to prevent a retailer with market power from raising prices.

83. Minimum resale price maintenance

(A) should be unlawful because it hurts consumers by preventing the entry of new firms that can provide the same good or service at a lower price.

(B) prevents the exercise of market power by dominant retailers.

(C) may be legal under a rule of reason if it is used to prevent free riding by cost cutting retailers and promoting investment in quality by retailers.

(D) is per se legal in a dual distributorship.

84. In order to establish an illegal vertical agreement,

(A) the antitrust plaintiff must show an express agreement.

(B) the antitrust plaintiff can show a tacit agreement through conscious parallelism.

(C) the antitrust plaintiff must show agreement as to a specific price and termination for failure to maintain price.

(D) the antitrust plaintiff can show threats to terminate a specific retailer who has violated the agreement.

85. A retailer is terminated by a manufacturer. The retailer claims that the termination was the result of an illegal maximum resale price maintenance agreement that the retailer did not follow. The retailer's suit

(A) will be successful if the agreement is in fact illegal.

    (B) will be unsuccessful if the agreement did not result in consumer harm.

    (C) will be successful if the maximum resale price maintenance agreement was not part of a scheme to restrict the number of retailers in a particular geographic area.

    (D) will be unsuccessful because the retailer has not plead an antitrust injury.

86.   Under the Supreme Court ruling in Business Electronics v. Sharp,

    (A) a vertical restraint is subject to the rule of reason.

    (B) a vertical restraint is not illegal per se unless it includes some agreement as to price or price level.

    (C) a vertical restraint is per se illegal if the manufacturer has market power and subject to the rule of reason otherwise.

    (D) a vertical restraint is subject to the rule of reason if the retailer lacks market power.

87.   All the retailers in a particular industry agree to not charge below a particular price. In bargaining with manufacturers, the individual retailers obtain a term in the contract requiring minimum resale price maintenance. Which of the following is true about this fact pattern?

    (A) The minimum resale price agreement is subject to the rule of reason despite the agreement among the retailers.

    (B) The agreement among the retailers will likely be subject to the per se rule against horizontal price fixing.

    (C) Because the agreement among the retailers is part of a set of vertical agreements, the retailers' agreement will be subject to the rule of reason.

    (D) The agreements are not subject to antitrust review because there is no antitrust injury.

88.   An agreement among manufacturers and retailers to create exclusive distribution systems that promote the provision of services and quality

    (A) would be legal because of the business justifications.

    (B) would be per se illegal because of the horizontal elements among manufacturers and among retailers.

    (C) would consist of both horizontal and vertical arrangements and both sets of agreements will have to be proven.

    (D) would be subject to the rule of reason because of the procompetitive goals of intrabrand competition.

89.   An exclusive dealership

(A) is an agreement that only one dealer, or retailer, will distribute the products or services of a manufacturer.

(B) may be considered legal because of the competition to be the exclusive dealer.

(C) Both A and B.

(D) Neither A nor B.

90. If a dominant dealer is made an exclusive dealer by forcing the manufacturer to terminate competing dealers,

(A) the agreement between the dealer and manufacturer is subject to the rule of reason.

(B) the agreement between the dealer and manufacturer is subject to the per se rule because the dealer is effectively eliminating direct competitors.

(C) the agreement is immune from the rule of Business Electronics v. Sharp because its existence is obvious.

(D) the agreement is immune from antitrust review because there is no antitrust injury.

91. Which of the following statements correctly describes the difference between an exclusive dealership and exclusive dealing?

(A) Exclusive dealership makes a specific manufacturer the sole provider of all of a specific retailer's requirements while an exclusive dealing arrangement requires a specific retailer to sell all the output of a specific manufacturer.

(B) Under an exclusive dealership, a specific retailer is the sole retailer for the manufacturer either in a particular region or globally. Under an exclusive dealing arrangement, a retailer agrees not to sell the output of any other manufacturer.

(C) Exclusive dealership is per se illegal while an exclusive dealing arrangement is subject to the rule of reason.

(D) While an exclusive dealership limits the retailer to a particular manufacturer, an exclusive dealing arrangement limits a manufacturer to a particular retailer.

92. An exclusive dealing arrangement is subject to review under

(A) the Sherman Act.

(B) the Clayton Act.

(C) the Federal Trade Commission Act.

(D) All of the above.

93. An exclusive dealing arrangement is subject to review under the Clayton Act if

(A) the arrangement covers the sale of a product which restraints trade.

(B) the arrangement covers the sale of a product or service that substantially lessens competition.

(C) the arrangement covers the sale of a product that substantially lessens competition.

(D) the arrangement covers the sale or purchase of a product that substantially lessens competition.

94. As applied to exclusive dealing arrangements, the difference between a claim under the Clayton Act and under the Sherman Act is

    (A) a claim under the Clayton Act applies only to an outputs contract.

    (B) a claim under the Clayton Act requires a showing that competition has been foreclosed while a claim under the Sherman Act requires rule of reason analysis.

    (C) a claim under the Clayton Act falls under the per se rule while a claim under the Sherman Act requires application of the rule of reason.

    (D) a claim under the Clayton Act does not require antitrust injury while a claim under the Sherman Act does not.

95. A tying arrangement

    (A) is a requirement that a purchaser obtain a second product or service when entering into a contract for a product or service.

    (B) is per se illegal under the Sherman Act and under the Clayton Act.

    (C) is subject to the rule of reason if there are economic efficiencies in the tying.

    (D) is subject to the per se rule if there are no economic efficiencies in the tying.

96. If there is market power in the tying product,

    (A) the per se rule applies.

    (B) rule of reason would still apply unless there is also market power in the tied product.

    (C) the antitrust plaintiff has made the case for an antitrust violation.

    (D) rule of reason applies.

97. Which of the following is a defense to a claim of tying?

    (A) The purchaser agreed to the tie.

    (B) The tie was demanded by the purchaser.

(C) The tying and tied products are actually one product or service.

(D) The defendant lacked market power at the time of the tying agreement.

98. In the United States v. Microsoft decision,

(A) the court ruled that Microsoft lacked market power and so there was no basis for a claim that Microsoft was engaged in an illegal tying agreement.

(B) the court ruled that Internet Explorer and Windows were one product.

(C) the court ruled that Microsoft had not engaged in illegal licensing practices.

(D) the court ruled that a rule of reason was the applicable standard for a software based tying arrangement.

SHORT ANSWER QUESTIONS: Please write a one paragraph response of about five to ten sentences to each of the following.

99. Explain the difference between a horizontal and vertical agreement and why antitrust law covers each.

ANSWER:

100. Explain whether this statement is accurate: vertical agreements are subject to the rule of reason because they are less harmful than horizontal ones.

ANSWER:

101. Which of the following is not an accurate statement about the differences between Section One and Section Two of the Sherman Act?

   (A) Section One covers agreements in restraint of trade while Section Two covers monopolization.

   (B) Section One requires proof of an agreement while Section Two requires proof of market power.

   (C) Section One violations can occur through conduct of one entity while Section Two violations can occur through conduct of one or more entities.

   (D) Section One violations can result in treble damage awards as can Section Two violations.

102. Which of the following is an accurate statement about Section Two of the Sherman Act?

   (A) Section Two requires a showing of intent to monopolize.

   (B) Section Two can base liability solely on the act of being a monopolist.

   (C) Section Two covers liability for the status monopolist.

   (D) Section Two requires a showing of market power.

103. Which of the following set of factors are relevant to market definition?

   (A) Geography, time, and market share of the defendant.

   (B) Time, ease of entry, and geography.

   (C) Concentration, number of firms, and customer base.

   (D) Price elasticity of demand, number of firms, and concentration.

104. The cross price elasticity between the demand for bicycles and the price of automobiles is positive. This means

   (A) bicycles and automobiles are complements.

   (B) bicycles and automobiles are in the same market.

(C) bicycles and automobiles are substitutes and may or may not be in the same market.

(D) very little because of the "Cellophane fallacy."

105. "An act that constitutes a Section One violation if done by two or more firms in concert would be a violation of Section Two if done unilaterally." This statement

(A) accurately states the current interpretation of the Sherman Act.

(B) inaccurately states the current law because it ignores the need to show intent for a Section Two violation.

(C) accurately states the law if the firm acting unilaterally is also a member of the cartel violating Section One.

(D) inaccurately states the law because the firm acting unilaterally may not have market power.

106. Which of the following acts may serve as a basis for a Section Two violation (assuming the firm has market power)?

(A) The firm lowers price to drive out competitors without a business justification.

(B) The firm acquires a set of patents to cover its technological advantage.

(C) The firm develops a sizable market share because consumers prefer its products over that of competitors.

(D) The firm exclusively licenses its patents to only one licensee.

107. In the Alcoa decision,

(A) Judge Hand included foreign supply of aluminum ingot in the relevant market.

(B) Judge Hand excluded the secondary market for aluminum ingot because Alcoa effectively had control for the second hand market.

(C) Judge Hand held that Alcoa's monopoly position was the result of "skill, foresight and industry."

(D) Judge hand held that Alcoa did not have the intent to monopolize.

108. A firm with market power that has excess capacity

(A) is in per se violation of Section Two of the Sherman Act.

(B) is in violation of Section One of the Sherman Act under the rule of reason.

(C) may be engaging in monopolistic conduct by foreclosing entry of new firms and reducing output in the market.

(D)   is demonstrating skill, foresight and industry in building its strong market position.

109. Which of the following is an accurate statement about market power and Section Two of the Sherman Act?

(A)   If the plaintiff's alleged injury is in a different market from the one in which the defendant has market power, there likely is no violation.

(B)   If the defendant had market power in the past but no longer has it, then the defendant is not liable.

(C)   If the defendant has obtained market power through skill, foresight, and industry, then there is no Section Two violation.

(D)   If the defendant faces potential competition in the future even though it has market power currently, there is no Section Two violation.

110. From an economic perspective, the problem with monopolization is

(A)   too many firms entering and flooding the marketplace with poor quality products.

(B)   deadweight loss arising from too little quantity and too high a price as compared to the perfectly competitive outcome.

(C)   loss of innovation incentive as the dominant firm lowers prices in order to prevent entry.

(D)   too low a price for a product resulting in too much entry.

111. A monopsony

(A)   is a market with one buyer and one seller.

(B)   is a market that results in too low a price and too much quantity because there is only one buyer.

(C)   is not actionable under the antitrust laws.

(D)   is liable without a showing of market power.

112. An industry with a few dominant firms with high barriers to entry

(A)   is effectively immune from the antitrust laws.

(B)   is the same as a monopoly even though it may be called an oligopoly since dominance is actionable under Section Two of the Sherman Act.

(C)   may be subject to antitrust scrutiny if there is an agreement among firms to engage in restraint of trade.

(D) is subject to the antitrust laws only if one of the dominant firms attempts to exclude the others and drive them out of the market.

113. An oligopoly

   (A) is subject to liability for its firms under Section Two of the Sherman Act.

   (B) may be held liable under the Federal Trade Commission Act.

   (C) would expose its firms to liability only under Section One of the Sherman Act.

   (D) generally is as efficient as a perfectly competitive market.

114. If a firm owns a patent or other intellectual property,

   (A) the firm is presumed to have market power under antitrust laws.

   (B) the firm is liable under Section Two of the Sherman Act if it has market power and engages in monopolistic conduct.

   (C) the firm violates Section Two of the Sherman Act upon a showing of market power alone.

   (D) the firm is immune from antitrust laws since intellectual property policy trumps antitrust law.

115. Which of the following are remedies for a violation of Section Two of the Sherman Act?

   (A) Divestiture, or break up, of the firm.

   (B) Treble damages.

   (C) Criminal penalties, such as incarceration.

   (D) All of the above.

SHORT ANSWER QUESTIONS: Please write a one paragraph response of about five to ten sentences to each of the following.

116. Compare and contrast Section One and Section Two claims under the Sherman Act.
ANSWER:

117. Explain market power and why it is an element of a Section Two claim.
ANSWER:

118. Which of the following is a true statement about a claim under Section Two of the Sherman Act?

    (A) Plaintiff must show that the defendant has market power and has conspired or entered into a contract to restrain trade.

    (B) Plaintiff must show that defendant has market power and need not show any bad act on the part of the defendant.

    (C) Plaintiff must show that the defendant has market power and has engaged in conduct that is exclusionary, predatory, or entails leveraging market power in one market into another.

    (D) Plaintiff must show that the defendant has market power and has engaged in business behavior that is economically inefficient.

119. Exclusionary conduct is one that

    (A) entails increasing barriers to entry that prevent competition.

    (B) entails using market power in one market to obtain power in another.

    (C) entails setting the market price with competitors.

    (D) entails requiring a purchaser to buy a separate product as a condition to buying another product.

120. Leveraging is conduct that

    (A) entails increasing barriers to entry that prevent competition.

    (B) entails using market power in one market to obtain power in another.

    (C) entails setting the market price with competitors.

    (D) entails requiring a purchaser to buy a separate product as a condition to buying another product.

121. The monopolistic conduct found in the Alcoa case was

    (A) the raising of the price of aluminum ingot by Alcoa in order to increase barriers to entry and exclude competition.

(B) the creation of excess capacity by Alcoa in order to predate the market and reduce competition.

(C) the use of market power in the market for aluminum ingot to obtain market power in the market for recycled aluminum.

(D) the agreement between Alcoa and its subsidiaries to fix price.

122. Which of the following is a criticism of Section Two of the Sherman Act?

(A) Section Two sometimes condemns conduct as monopolistic which benefits consumers.

(B) Section Two sometimes strikes down agreements that might enhance market competition by preventing free riding.

(C) Section Two sometimes condemns monopolies that are efficient joint ventures.

(D) Section Two sometimes condemns vertical restraints that enhance interbrand competition.

123. The monopolistic conduct found in the United Shoe case was

(A) requiring licensees of the company's shoe manufacturing equipment to buy the leather used to make shoes.

(B) allowing licensees to only license but never purchase machine equipment.

(C) threatening potential entrants in the market for shoes with high prices for equipment.

(D) not permitting repair services for machines from independent service providers.

124. The conduct at issue in Berkey Photo v. Kodak was

(A) the leveraging of market power in the market for film to obtain a monopoly in the market for cameras.

(B) the predisclosure by a company that had market power in the market for film of a new type of film incompatible with existing cameras.

(C) the creation of a camera loaded with film by a company that had market power in the market for film.

(D) the cutting of price for cameras by a company that had market power in the market for film.

125. A firm with market power that creates a new and innovative technology

(A) will be liable under Section Two of the Sherman Act.

(B)   may be liable if there is a dangerous probability of gaining market power in the new technology.

(C)   is never liable since the Sherman Act has as one of its goals the creation of more efficient technologies.

(D)   may be liable if the new technology does not result in a superior product and lower prices and there is additional abusive conduct by the firm.

126.   A firm refuses to supply an input or otherwise cooperate with a rival in the marketplace. Which of the following is an inaccurate statement based on this fact?

(A)   The firm will not be liable under Section Two of the Sherman Act if the firm lacks market power.

(B)   The firm has a duty to cooperate under Section Two of the Sherman Act if the firm has market power.

(C)   The firm may be liable under Section Two of the Sherman Act if it has market power and its refusal to deal is part of an existing agreement to cooperate with the rival.

(D)   The firm may be liable under Section Two of the Sherman Act if it has market power and there is no business justification for the refusal to deal.

127.   The essential facilities doctrine

(A)   is an often applied basis for a Section Two claim after the United States Supreme Court decision in United States v. Terminal Railway 1912.

(B)   is based on a duty to cooperate with rivals based on the United States Supreme Court decision in Aspen Skiing Co. v. Aspen Highlands 1985.

(C)   may be applicable if a firm with market power denies access to a facility that cannot be readily duplicated and could feasibly be provided.

(D)   is the basis for exempting owners of intellectual property from antitrust laws.

128.   A firm with market power moves into retailing and distribution. Subsequently, the firm refuses to deal with other independently owned retailers in the supply of a product or service. Which of the following is a true statement based on these facts?

(A)   The dominant firm's conduct is not a violation of Section Two of the Sherman Act because vertical integration leads to more efficient firms.

(B)   The dominant firm is liable under Section Two of the Sherman Act since market power is now being extended into retailing and distribution.

(C)   The dominant firm is not liable under Section Two of the Sherman Act unless the product or service denied constitutes an essential facility.

(D) The dominant firm may be liable under Section Two of the Sherman Act if competition is lessened in the retailing and distribution market.

129. Vertical integration, the merger or acquisition of firms at different stages in the marketing and distribution chain, is

  (A) per se legal under Section Two of the Sherman Act because such mergers or acquisitions yield efficiency.

  (B) actionable under Section Two of the Sherman Act since vertical integration can foreclose competition and reduce the number of firms in a market.

  (C) not actionable under Section Two of the Sherman Act because vertical integration reduces transaction costs resulting in savings that can be passed on to consumers.

  (D) actionable under Section Two of the Sherman Act because it lowers barriers to entry and thereby facilitates the creation of market power.

130. A firm owns forests to produce raw lumber which in turn is used to make housing materials. The firm raises the price of raw lumber it sells to competitors and lowers the price of the housing materials, the final product made using raw lumber. Which of the following is an inaccurate statement based on these facts?

  (A) The firm is engaging in a price squeeze.

  (B) The firm's liability under the Sherman Act will be based on whether its conduct is predatory in the market for housing materials.

  (C) The firm is not liable since competitors can refuse to deal and not buy the lumber.

  (D) The firm is not liable if the lowering of the price in the market for housing materials does not tend to monopolize the market.

131. A price squeeze

  (A) results in lower prices and therefore cannot constitute a violation of the Sherman Act.

  (B) might be actionable if market power in one market is being leveraged in another market.

  (C) might be actionable if the price squeeze is predatory.

  (D) results in higher prices and therefore would constitute monopolistic conduct.

132. In Otter Tail v. United States, the United States Supreme Court upheld liability for Otter Tail because

  (A) Otter Tail was monopolizing an essential facility.

  (B) Otter Tail was tying sale of electricity to the provision of servicing electrical lines.

(C) Otter Tail was foreclosing entry and limiting competition as a vertically integrated firm.

(D) Otter Tail's price squeeze violated its duty to cooperate with competitors.

133. As a result of telephone deregulation, in the current telecommunications industry

(A) antitrust claims in the deregulated telephone industry are easier to bring since antitrust is needed to maintain competition in an industry previously regulated by the government.

(B) antitrust claims are more difficult to bring because of the Twombly decision requiring antitrust claims of conspiracy to be plausible and because of the Trinko decision limiting Section Two claims.

(C) antitrust claims are more difficult to bring because Congress expressly does not allow for antitrust claims under the Telecommunications Act of 1996.

(D) antitrust claims are easier to bring because in a deregulated industry, antitrust is the main means to maintain competition.

134. Raising rivals' cost

(A) is a theory of Section Two that explains leveraging behavior but does not explain exclusionary behavior.

(B) is per se legal as effective competition.

(C) can explain the result in Aspen Skiing and Otter Tail as theories of exclusionary conduct.

(D) is the theory adopted by the Supreme Court in the Microsoft decision.

135. In United States v. Microsoft,

(A) the court found that Microsoft lacked market power because in a dynamic industry there is potential competition from new operating systems.

(B) the court found that Internet Explorer and Windows were one integrated product and there was no basis for a tying claim.

(C) the court developed a standard based on reasonableness, rather than a per se analysis, in assessing ties involving software.

(D) the court held that technological ties are exclusionary and entail leveraging.

136. A tying arrangement

(A) is actionable only under Section Two of the Sherman Act as monopolistic conduct.

(B) is not actionable if the two products are technological complements.

(C)   is subject to per se analysis if there is market power in the tying product.

(D)   is not actionable unless there is market power in the tied product.

137. Which of the following is not an example of a potentially actionable tying arrangement?

(A)   A requirement to buy printer cartridges as a condition of leasing a printer.

(B)   A requirement to buy branded napkins and condiment packages as a condition of entering a fast food franchise.

(C)   A requirement to obtain service from an authorized repair company as a condition of leasing business laptops.

(D)   A requirement to obtain financing only from the seller as a condition of buying a rubber manufacturing machine.

138. A patent owner licenses a patented process for making chemical dyes. A condition of this license is that the licensee buys all the chemicals he requires to practice the process from the patent owner. Which of the following is a true statement based on these facts?

(A)   The condition constitutes a technological tie and is per se illegal under Section Two of the Sherman Act.

(B)   The condition does not constitute a tie because the chemicals and the process are one product.

(C)   The condition constitutes a per se illegal tying arrangement because ownership of the patent constitutes market power.

(D)   The condition may constitute a tying arrangement but is not per se illegal unless the patent owner has market power in the process.

139. The practice of block booking used in the early years of the motion picture industry

(A)   was an example of a tying arrangement.

(B)   was an example of an essential facility.

(C)   was an example of predation by the motion picture studios.

(D)   was an example of a per se legal practice under Section Two of the Sherman Act.

140. A monopsony is a market with a single buyer and

(A)   is exempt from antitrust review.

(B)   is actionable under a lower standard because a monopsonist results in lower prices, which is beneficial to consumers.

(C) can result in anticompetitive conditions since lowering prices for inputs can result in lower quantity of inputs and outputs.

(D) is generally beneficial to consumers.

141. Pricing by a monopolist or a monopsonist

(A) is anticompetitive and can result in liability under Section Two of the Sherman Act.

(B) is not actionable by itself unless accompanied by some monopolistic conduct.

(C) results in inefficiencies that the Sherman Act corrects.

(D) is rarely actionable since pricing is the product of effective private bargaining.

142. Market power for a monopsonist depends upon

(A) the number of competing buyers, geography, and time.

(B) the price elasticity of demand for the product.

(C) the markup between price and marginal cost.

(D) the ability to lower price below average variable cost.

SHORT ANSWER QUESTIONS: Please write a one paragraph response of about five to ten sentences to each of the following.

143. Monopolistic conduct is divided into three types: exclusionary, predatory, and leveraging. Briefly explain each.

ANSWER:

144. Explain the policy reasons for why antitrust law prohibits monopolistic conduct but not monopolies as such.

ANSWER:

TOPIC 8:
ATTEMPTED MONOPOLIZATION

145. To make a claim for attempted monopolization, the plaintiff must show

   (A) conduct by the defendant and a dangerous probability that the conduct is predatory.

   (B) conduct showing a specific intent to monopolize and a dangerous probability that the monopolization will be successful.

   (C) conduct showing gross recklessness in monopolization and a dangerous probability that the conduct will be successful.

   (D) specific intent to monopolize and a dangerous probability that the monopolization will be successful.

146. Which of the following is an inaccurate statement about specific intent in an attempted monopolization claim?

   (A) Pricing practices showing a predatory purpose can be evidence of specific intent.

   (B) Subjective hopes that a competitor will not do well can establish specific intent.

   (C) A pattern of not dealing with competitors and denying access to essential facilities can establish specific intent.

   (D) Mere vigorous competition and a desire to do better than one's rivals are not sufficient to establish specific intent.

147. Which of the following is an accurate statement about an attempted monopolization claim?

   (A) If there is a high dangerous probability of success, then the plaintiff does not need to prove specific intent.

   (B) A showing of strong specific intent is sufficient to establish a dangerous probability of success.

   (C) If there is clear evidence of specific intent, then conduct need not be shown.

   (D) Dangerous probability of success and specific intent have to be established separately.

148. Market definition

(A) is not necessary for an attempted monopolization claim since there need not be evidence of market power.

(B) is relevant in order to establish dangerous probability of success.

(C) is not necessary if there is strong evidence of specific intent.

(D) is relevant to determine the specific intent of the defendant.

149. Market share analysis in an attempted monopolization case

(A) can serve as a proxy for dangerous probability of success in measuring how close the defendant is to having a dominant position in the market.

(B) provides strong evidence of specific intent and improper conduct by the defendant.

(C) can demonstrate the adverse effects on consumers from defendant's conduct.

(D) can help to establish the market power element of an attempted monopolization claim.

150. A leveraging theory in an attempted monopolization claim

(A) arises when a firm engages in predatory conduct involving below cost pricing.

(B) arises when a firm with market power in one market is engaging conduct that allows extension of market power into related markets.

(C) arises when a firm fails to cooperate with a rival.

(D) arises when a firm with market power attempts to prevent the entry of new firms.

151. Which of the following is a true statement about a predatory pricing theory of attempted monopolization?

(A) Predatory pricing is the claim that a dominant firm is cutting its price in order to obtain market power in a market for a related product or service.

(B) Predatory pricing is a claim that can be established by showing that prices have been low and unchanging over a long period of time.

(C) Predatory pricing is a claim which, in order to be plausible, must include some evidence that the predating firm can recoup its losses in the future.

(D) Predatory pricing is a claim that is inherently implausible because low prices help consumers and firms can readily enter a market.

152. The economics of predatory pricing

(A) requires pricing below marginal cost and ability to raise price to deter entry.

   (B) predicts that predatory pricing will work if demand is relatively inelastic with respect to its own price.

   (C) requires pricing at the profit maximizing level and large barriers to entry in a market.

   (D) predicts that predatory pricing will not work if a firm has excess capacity.

153. Which of the following would make it more likely that predatory pricing will be successful?

   (A) Very little excess capacity for the firm attempting to predate.

   (B) Plants and equipment currently being unused by the firm attempting to predate.

   (C) Ease of entry by competitors to the firm attempting to predate.

   (D) Few substitutes and lowered price elasticity of demand in the market that the firm is attempting to predate.

154. Which of the following can be evidence relevant to a predatory pricing claim?

   (A) Price below total cost.

   (B) Price below average variable cost.

   (C) Price equal to marginal cost but below average variable cost.

   (D) Price equal to average variable cost but below marginal cost.

155. The Areeda-Turner measure of price and cost as evidence in a predatory pricing case

   (A) is problematic because marginal cost is impossible to measure.

   (B) may capture situations where a firm is engaging in limiting pricing that may actually be beneficial to the marketplace.

   (C) may make it more difficult for a predating firm to recoup lost profits.

   (D) ensures that efficient predation is not deterred while allowing for identification of predatory firms that have a dangerous probability of success.

156. A predatory buying claim

   (A) is held to a different legal standard than a predatory pricing claim.

   (B) entails a buyer paying below cost in the hope of obtaining deeper discounts in the future.

   (C) entails a buyer overbidding in order to obtain a dominant position that would allow obtaining lower price for inputs as a monopsonist.

   (D) is less easy to establish than a predatory pricing claim.

157. A firm bundles several separate products into one package and sells the entire package at an allegedly low price with the specific intent to drive out competitors. Such a practice, known as discounted bundles,

   (A) is not a violation of the antitrust laws.

   (B) is analyzed under the rule of reason to see whether the firm bundles the products more efficiently than competitors.

   (C) is considered a form of predatory pricing but there is disagreement on the appropriate comparison of price and cost.

   (D) is per se illegal because bundling itself forecloses competition.

158. A conspiracy to monopolize

   (A) falls under the dangerous probability of success standard of Spectrum Sports.

   (B) can be established through conduct and specific intent.

   (C) can be established through an agreement, overt act, and specific intent.

   (D) is identical to a Section One claim of agreement to restrain trade.

159. In a predatory pricing case, the plaintiff is able to show that the defendant priced at 10 % below its average variable cost for two years. Which of the following is an accurate statement based on this fact?

   (A) The plaintiff has made a prima facie case to withstand summary judgment.

   (B) The plaintiff still must show specific intent.

   (C) The plaintiff must show that the defendant would have been able to maintain a monopoly after obtaining a dominant position in the market.

   (D) The plaintiff has met its prima facie case with the burden shifting to the defendant to show business justifications for the price cutting.

SHORT ANSWER QUESTIONS: Please write a one paragraph response of about five to ten sentences to each of the following.

160. Explain the relevance of market power to an attempted monopolization claim.

ANSWER:

161. Explain the claim of predatory pricing and a criticism of such a claim.

ANSWER:

162. Which of the following statements about mergers and acquisitions is accurate?

    (A) A horizontal merger tends to lead to market concentration while a vertical merger helps firms to realize cost saving and efficiencies.

    (B) Both horizontal and vertical mergers can foreclose competition.

    (C) Conglomerate mergers tend to help firms realize efficiencies across different markets with little effect on market foreclosure.

    (D) Both horizontal and vertical mergers lead to efficiencies that outweigh anticompetitive effects.

163. Under the Sherman Act,

    (A) mergers and acquisitions were seen as per se violations until courts moved to a rule of reason.

    (B) courts adopted a deferential standard to mergers and acquisitions until Section Seven of the Clayton Act heighted judicial scrutiny.

    (C) rule of reason applied to vertical mergers and per se analysis applied to horizontal mergers.

    (D) only an acquisition constituted an antitrust violation because a merger was not a contract or combination.

164. Under Section Seven of the Clayton Act as originally enacted,

    (A) vertical mergers were given higher judicial scrutiny than horizontal mergers.

    (B) stock purchases were actionable but not purchases of assets.

    (C) a plaintiff had to show a dangerous probability of success.

    (D) Congress enacted a lenient rule of reason approach to merger analysis adopting the standard then existing under the Sherman Act.

165. The Celler-Kefauver Amendments to Section Seven of the Clayton Act

    (A) lowered the standard for review of horizontal mergers.

    (B) gave the Federal Trade Commission jurisdiction over merger review.

    (C) made both horizontal and vertical mergers unlawful upon a showing of a reasonable probability of anticompetitive effects.

    (D) required the Department of Justice and the Federal Trade Commission to examine efficiencies before granting approval to a merger.

166. Under the Clayton Act,

    (A) a private party cannot challenge a merger or acquisition.

    (B) a private party in some situations can obtain a remedy of divestiture if the plaintiff can show threatened loss or damage to person interests.

    (C) a suit by the United States Department of Justice or the Federal Trade Commission would preclude a private party action.

    (D) a private party can obtain treble damages but not an injunction.

167. Hart-Scott-Rodino

    (A) is the section of the Sherman Act enacted in 1890 to govern mergers.

    (B) is a 1976 statute that amended the Clayton Act to require companies intended to merger to give notification to the government.

    (C) raised the standard for merger review to a quick look rule of reason subject to efficiency defenses.

    (D) gave the Department of Justice authority to divest a company of its assets.

168. Under Hart-Scott-Rodino,

    (A) the Department of Justice is given precomplaint discovery powers to investigate a merger.

    (B) requires companies to give premerger notification if the merger or acquisition exceeds a certain dollar value.

    (C) allows state attorney generals to challenge mergers or acquisitions.

    (D) All of the above.

169. The failing company defense

    (A) allows a merger to go through if the parties can show that one of companies in the merger is bankrupt.

    (B) is available as a defense if the HHI of the two combined firms does not rise above a certain percentage.

(C)   is available as a defense if one of the companies faced the grave risk of business failure and would not be purchased by a noncompetitor.

(D)   allows a merger to be challenged if one of the firms in the merger was failing because of mismanagement and inefficiencies.

170. Two firms do not compete currently in the market for electric car batteries. They seek to form a joint venture to enter the market. If the joint venture is allowed, it would have a dominant market share in the market for electric car batteries. Which of the following is an accurate statement based on these facts?

(A)   The merger is per se lawful since the joint venture is a new entrant in the market and therefore promotes competition.

(B)   The merger is unlawful if the entrants would not have entered the market independently or the entry would not have made the market less concentrated.

(C)   The merger is unlawful if the efficiency gains of the merger are outweighed by the efficiency losses.

(D)   The merger is lawful if the competitive gains outweigh the competitive losses.

171. The Herfindahl-Hirschman Index (HHI) measures market concentration by adding

(A)   the price elasticity of demand and the price elasticity of supply.

(B)   the market share of each firm in the industry measured at the same time.

(C)   the changes in the market share of firms in an industry over time.

(D)   the square of the market share of each in the industry measured at the same time.

172. After a proposed, the HHI will go from 1600 to 2000. This means

(A)   the market will remain slightly concentrated before and after the merger.

(B)   the market will remain highly concentrated before and after the merger.

(C)   the market will change from slightly concentrated to highly concentrated before and after the merger.

(D)   the market will remain unconcentrated before and after the merger.

173. If the post merger HHI is 1500 and the change in HHI before and after the merger is 50,

(A)   the merger is unlikely to be challenged.

(B)   the merger is likely to be challenged.

(C)   the merger will be subject to strict scrutiny.

(D) the merger is unlikely to be challenged if the firms can show efficiency benefits.

174. In analyzing market power under the Department of Justice Merger Guidelines,

(A) the HHI serves as the best indicator of a firm's ability to set price.

(B) the agency will consider demand and supply elasticity to gauge how consumers and firms would respond to changes in price.

(C) the Cellophane Fallacy has been abrogated through regulation.

(D) the agency will consider geographic markets but not potential competition.

175. In gauging barriers to entry in a market under the Merger Guidelines,

(A) the agency will ignore the effect of returns to scale on entry of new firms.

(B) the agency will consider solely the process by which firms enter and ignore technological barriers.

(C) the agency will examine whether firms will enter if there is a significant but nontransitory increase in price.

(D) the agency will focus on how the HHI responds to a more equitable market division of the market.

176. Which of the following is an accurate statement about the role of efficiencies in merger analysis under the Merger Guidelines?

(A) The possibility of efficiencies through mergers makes most mergers legal.

(B) Efficiencies that arise as a result of the merger are a consideration on judging the legality of the merger.

(C) Efficiencies can be presumed from the existence of technologies, economies of scale, and intellectual property.

(D) Efficiencies must have greater benefits than the anticompetitive harms for the merger to be approved.

SHORT ANSWER QUESTIONS: Please write a one paragraph response of about five to ten sentences to each of the following.

177. Explain why merger and acquisitions are subject to review under the antitrust laws.
ANSWER:

178. Explain the costs and benefits of corporate mergers and acquisitions.
ANSWER:

179. Which of the following is an accurate statement about the economics of price discrimination?

    (A) A firm price discriminates when it sells products of different quality at different prices.

    (B) A firm price discriminates when it sells product of identical quality at different prices at different points in time.

    (C) A firm price discriminates when it advertises a price and then gives discounts to all purchasers.

    (D) A firm price discriminates when it sells goods of identical quality at different prices to different consumers.

180. Which of the following is an inaccurate statement about the economics of price discrimination?

    (A) A firm engaging in first degree price discrimination can lead to social welfare maximization with the firm obtaining the consumer and producer surplus in the market.

    (B) A firm engaging in second degree price discrimination can lead to improvements in social welfare if the firm sells more output than what it would sell if it did not price discriminate.

    (C) A firm engaging in third degree price discrimination may either worsen or improve social welfare.

    (D) Price discrimination provides firms with greater business flexibility and therefore maximizes social welfare.

181. A firm sells a business version of software for $ 300 and a university version for $ 20. Which of the following is true about this fact?

    (A) The firm is engaging in price discrimination if the business version has more features than the university version.

    (B) If the two versions have the same features, then the firm is engaging in first degree price discrimination.

(C) The firm is engaging in second degree price discrimination if both versions have the same features and both business and university purchasers buy the same number of software packages.

(D) Third degree price discrimination is present if the two versions have identical features.

182. The purpose of the Robinson-Patman Act was to

   (A) allow large national firms to compete more effectively at the global level.

   (B) prevent smaller firms from colluding to form national chains.

   (C) prevent large national firms from treating customers differently in order to drive out smaller firms that could not offer attractive deals.

   (D) allow customers to have recourse if firms set different price terms based on immutable characteristics of customers.

183. Antitrust injury under the Robinson-Patman Act consists of

   (A) primary line injury to the customers of the discriminating firm.

   (B) secondary line injury to the competitors of the discriminating firm.

   (C) tertiary line injury to the customers buying from customers of the discriminating firm.

   (D) any injury to person or property that arises from an anticompetitive practice.

184. A criticism of the Robinson-Patman Act is

   (A) civil rights laws better deal with discriminating behavior with respect to price.

   (B) the act sometimes finds illegal conduct that benefits consumers.

   (C) price discrimination is a practice that benefits competition.

   (D) the costs of enforcement include detecting behavior that cannot be observed.

185. A defense to a Robinson-Patman claim includes

   (A) lowering price in good faith to meet the price of a competitor.

   (B) products and services are of different grade or quality.

   (C) price reflects differences in costs.

   (D) All of the above.

186. A claim of price predation under the Robinson-Patman Act

(A) is easier to establish than under Section Two of the Sherman Act since the plaintiff only has to show that there was a price difference in identical goods that is not cost justified.

(B) is difficult since, among other elements, the plaintiff has to show a reasonable prospect of recoupment by the discriminating firm.

(C) is easier to establish than under Section Two of the Sherman Act since the plaintiff has to show that only one of the two prices is below average variable cost.

(D) is difficult since the plaintiff has to show special antitrust injury above the usual elements for a claim of price predation under Section Two of the Sherman Act.

187. Firms often use a system of base point pricing where prices are calculated based on a uniform point of sale or delivery as opposed to charging prices based on the buyer's cost of shipping. Such a system of base point pricing

(A) is per se illegal under the Robinson-Patman Act.

(B) is defensible under the Robinson-Patman Act since the price differences reflect the cost of shipping to the seller.

(C) is defensible under the Robinson-Patman Act since the delivered price is the basis for determining price discrimination and the delivered price reflects the cost to the buyer.

(D) is illegal under the Robinson-Patman Act because the price does not reflect cost and does not serve to meet the competition.

188. Which of the following would be an example of a practice that would constitute price discrimination?

(A) Charging different ticket prices depending on where one sits in a theater and when one attends.

(B) Selling a new release of a DVD of a movie at a higher price during the first few months and then dropping the price.

(C) Selling a hardback and paperback book at different prices.

(D) Giving different buyers different time periods within which to respond to an advertised price discount.

189. Injury in a secondary-line price discrimination case consists of

(A) increased profits and unjust enrichment of the favored buyers.

(B) substantial price differences among buyers.

(C) increased profits of the price discriminator.

(D) cost savings that are passed on to customers.

190. Quantity discounts to retailers

(A) is actionable if the quantity discounts can be recouped in the future.

(B) may not be actionable if the discounts are due recognition and reimbursement for marketing functions.

(C) are actionable even if not substantial as a per se violation.

(D) are not actionable since there is no discrimination as to price.

191. If a seller attempts to meet competition, but ends up drastically cutting the price of a product sold to one buyer beyond what is charged to other buyers,

(A) the seller is liable under the Robinson-Patman Act.

(B) the seller is not liable if acting in good faith to meet the competition.

(C) the seller is liable if the price is below average variable cost.

(D) the seller is not liable even if not acting in good faith to meet the competition.

192. Which of the following statement is accurate with respect to the Robinson-Patman Act?

(A) The Robinson-Patman Act is unnecessary because price discrimination improves social welfare.

(B) The Robinson-Patman Act is unnecessary because it duplicates Section One of the Sherman Act.

(C) The Robinson-Patman Act was enacted to limit the power of monopolists in engaging in predatory behavior.

(D) The Robinson-Patman Act was enacted to limit the power of large chain stores getting discounts from suppliers and thereby obtaining an advantage over smaller retailers.

193. Which of the following pieces of information would aid a firm in engaging in price discrimination?

(A) Ability to distinguish among buyers and prevention of resale of the product.

(B) Knowledge of the costs of production of competitors.

(C) Willingness to pay among some buyers and availability of alternate sources of supply of the product.

(D) The relationship between price and average variable cost.

SHORT ANSWER QUESTIONS: Please write a one paragraph response of about five to ten sentences to each of the following.

194. Explain the concept of price discrimination and why antitrust law is concerned with the practice.

ANSWER:

195. Explain the benefits and costs of the practice of price discrimination.

ANSWER:

PRACTICE FINAL EXAM: QUESTIONS

Questions 196 to 200 are based on the following facts.

The market for sports drink consists of several firms. A group of five of these firms use a juice extracted from the agave cactus as a key ingredient in the drink. Agave cactus is very hard to obtain in the United States, but there is an active market globally for the juice. The five firms using agave decide to form a trade association for the purpose of negotiating a good price for the juice on the international market. The association is name Agave Purchasing Association (APA). The APA shares information about prices on agave and names of traders that sell the juice on the global market. They do not share price information about the sports drink that each firm makes using the agave. The APA negotiates a standard contract with a trader. The contract contains terms pertaining to the quality of agave, delivery, and price at which the firms buy the juice. Members of APA are told to avoid any trader that refuses to sign the standard contract of the APA.

196. The APA

   (A)   is unlikely to be liable under Section One or Section Two of the Sherman Act since it represents only five firms and is unlikely to have market power.

   (B)   is an example of a monopsony which is exempted from the antitrust laws.

   (C)   is an example of a joint venture subject to the rule of reason.

   (D)   is likely to be in violation of Section One of the Sherman Act as a price fixing combination.

197. The refusal to deal with non-cooperating traders

   (A)   is likely a violation of Section One of the Sherman Act as a group boycott.

   (B)   is not a violation of the Sherman Act since there is no duty to cooperate under the law.

   (C)   is not a violation of the Sherman Act but could be a violation of the Clayton Act if there is a dangerous probability of success as to monopolization.

   (D)   is likely a violation of Section One of the Sherman Act under a rule of reason analysis.

198. The agreement among the firms to form APA and the agreements with the traders are

   (A)   both examples of horizontal agreements.

   (B)   both examples of vertical agreements.

   (C)   subject to per se treatment as a horizontal agreement.

(D) subject to rule of reason treatment as a vertical agreement.

199. Suppose APA agrees to pay an above market price for the agave juice and requires the traders to supply all their output to members of the APA. Such an agreement

(A) is predatory per se.

(B) may be the basis for a claim of predatory pricing if there is market power and a possibility of recoupment if competitors are driven out of the market.

(C) is not actionable under Section Two of the Sherman Act since the APA is not one entity.

(D) is not actionable under Section One of the Sherman Act since the APA is one entity.

200. Suppose a current member of the APA refuses to comply with the association's terms and enters into an independent agreement with a trader to purchase agave juice. Which of the following is an accurate statement based on these facts?

(A) The independent firm might be in violation of Section Two if it has market power.

(B) The independent firm might be in violation of Section One because of the vertical restraint with the trader.

(C) The APA and its members might be liable under either Section Two or Section One if there is an agreement among the four remaining firms forcing traders not to deal with the independent firm.

(D) There is no potential liability under these facts since parties are free to contract with whomever they want.

Questions 201 to 206 are based on the following facts.

Peripheral is a company that designs and sells gaming equipment for game systems. It has recently patented a new type of controller that operates by placing the device over a player's index finger. The player can use the device when worn to control games on a tablet computer. Peripheral licenses the finger device to manufacturers of smart phones. As a condition of its license, Peripheral requires the manufacturers to buy a special, unpatented battery from Peripheral. In addition, the licensee must use copyrighted software written by Peripheral. The software is pre-installed on the finger device. Consumers who buy the table can obtain a separate license to buy and use the finger device from the seller of the smart phone. Peripheral requires any licensee selling the finger device to do so for at least $ 75.

201. Suppose a customer buying the smart phone challenges the contract between Peripheral and the smart phone manufacturers as an illegal tying agreement. Which of the following is an inaccurate statement based on these facts?

(A) It is very likely that the consumer will not have standing to bring the law suit.

(B) Peripheral, as patent owner, is presumed to have market power.

    (C) A defense to the claim of an illegal tie is that the software and the finger device together constitute one product.

    (D) The tying arrangement is subject to per se treatment if Peripheral has market power in the finger device.

202. Suppose the customer brings suit to challenge the price floor of $ 75. Which of the following is a true statement?

    (A) The customer will not have standing since it is an indirect purchaser.

    (B) The price floor is subject to per se treatment.

    (C) The price floor will be upheld if it's reasonable.

    (D) The price floor will be upheld unless Peripheral has market power in the finger device market.

203. Suppose a smart phone manufacturer begins to use its own batteries in the finger device. Peripheral threatens to discontinue supplying the manufacturer with the device unless it stops using its own battery. Which of the following is true?

    (A) Peripheral will most likely not be liable under Section Two since there is no duty to cooperate with a competitor or to license one's intellectual property.

    (B) Peripheral will be liable only if actually terminates the manufacturer.

    (C) The manufacturer does not have standing to sue since there is no antitrust injury.

    (D) The manufacturer will prevail if Peripheral has market power.

204. Suppose a manufacturer sells the device for less than $ 75. Peripheral refuses to further supply the manufacturer, who sues to challenge the price floor as a restraint of trade. The manufacturer of the smart phone

    (A) will prevail because of the price fixing.

    (B) will prevail if it can establish that the restraint was unreasonable.

    (C) will lose since it lacks standing.

    (D) will lose since there is not antitrust injury.

205. Suppose a manufacturer claims that Peripheral is engaging in a technological tie by designing a finger device to be used only with a particular kind of battery. This claim

    (A) will be successful since Peripheral is presumed to have market power.

    (B) will be unsuccessful if there are efficiencies in the design of the device and battery.

    (C) will be successful if the battery and device are two products.

(D) will be unsuccessful since the battery and device are one product.

206. Which of the following is an accurate statement about the economics of antitrust law?

(A) Economic theory would support broad enforcement of Section Two claims because monopolization is economically inefficient and reduces wealth.

(B) Economic theory would support treatment of most, if not all, vertical restraints under a rule of reason analysis.

(C) Economic theory supports the rationale for the Robinson-Patman Act, namely the protection of small retailers against large chain stores.

(D) Economic theory would support predatory pricing claims but only if the claim is based on evidence that the defendant priced below average variable cost.

207. Price discrimination

(A) can maximize the gains to consumer only if the discriminating firm can identify and charge the willingness to pay of each consumer in the marketplace.

(B) is illustrated by charging bulk buyers a lower price than purchasers who buy a single quantity.

(C) generally serves to promote efficiency but only if the product can be resold after the sale by the discriminating firm.

(D) is often associated with predatory behavior by buyers and therefore is per se illegal.

208. Which of the following is an inaccurate statement about per se rules and rule of reason under Section One of the Sherman Act?

(A) Price fixing among competitors is per se illegal.

(B) Division of territories among competitors is per se illegal.

(C) Proof of agreement can be shown from conduct that is parallel among competitors.

(D) Setting minimum resale prices is a per se violation.

209. A plaintiff pleads a claim of predatory pricing under Section Two of the Sherman Act. In addition, the pleadings include a claim that various firms in the market colluded to establish barriers to entry that would likely lead to a monopoly. Which of the following is an accurate statement about these facts?

(A) The claim of collusion has to be plausible under Trinko, and the predatory pricing claim is subject to per se treatment if the plaintiff can show price was below average variable cost for a sustained period of time.

(B) The claim of collusion will likely be dismissed for failure to state a claim of the agreement is not plausible, and the predatory pricing claim might be dismissed on a summary judgment motion if there is no evidence of recoupment.

(C) The claim of collusion will likely survive a summary judgment motion since there will be disputed facts about the existence of an agreement, and the predatory pricing claim will be dismissed for failure to state a claim.

(D) The claim of collusion will be dismissed for failure to state a claim, and the predatory pricing claim will survive a summary judgment motion since there will be disputed facts as to recoupment.

210. A market has an HHI of 1500 and a proposed merger would result in an increase in the HHI of 75 points. The proposed merger

(A) will be challenged by either the Department of Justice or the Federal Trade Commission.

(B) will be immune from challenge from either agency.

(C) will be given a quick look review by either agency.

(D) will fall in the area of suspect merger, but will likely survive review.

211. Which of the following is an accurate statement about an oligopoly market?

(A) Since an oligopoly consists of a few firms engaged in competition, a firm in an oligopoly market will be subject to extensive antitrust review.

(B) Since an oligopoly will have low barriers to entry, the risk of monopolization is low.

(C) Since an oligopoly has few firms, collusive behavior may be easier to sustain.

(D) Since an oligopoly has few firms, competition will most likely not be based on price, but on the quality of the product or service being provided.

212. A firm sues a competitor over a debt. The suit results in a settlement. Which of the following is an accurate statement about these facts?

(A) The suit is likely not to be found to be anticompetitive if the firm acted without malice.

(B) The suit itself can serve as a basis for an antitrust claim by the competitor if the suit was objectively baseless.

(C) The suit itself is likely not to be found to be anticompetitive if there was an objective basis for the suit or the firm acted thinking there was a basis for the suit.

(D) The suit's success depends on whether antitrust law preempts debtor-creditor law.

213. A firm petitions a zoning board to change a building restriction that would affect the plans of a competitor to expand its business. Which of the following is an accurate statement

based on these facts?

(A) The firm's action is a per se violation of the Sherman Act.

(B) The firm's action is immune from antitrust review because the petition of the zoning board is a legal act.

(C) The firm's action may be immune unless that petition was a sham.

(D) The firm's action will be immune since there is active supervision of the zoning board by the state.

214. Which of the following is an inaccurate statement about the relationship between antitrust law and regulated industries?

(A) A regulated industry may be immune from the antitrust laws under the governing statute.

(B) A deregulated industry, like telecommunications, will be subject to antitrust claims since government regulation no longer serves to ensure competition.

(C) A regulated industry may not be subject to antitrust review to avoid conflict between different government agencies.

(D) A deregulated industry is immune from antitrust review because Congress has made the decision to remove all government review from the industry.

215. Which of the following is an inaccurate statement about the relationship between antitrust law and intellectual property?

(A) Ownership of a copyright or patent does not exempt a firm from antitrust review.

(B) Ownership of a patent creates a presumption of market power for a tying claim.

(C) The DOJ Guidelines on Intellectual Property Licensing would subject most licenses to a rule of reason analysis.

(D) The DOJ Guidelines on Intellectual Property Licensing emphasize the procompetitive benefits of copyrights and patents.

Questions 216 to 220 are based on the following facts.

In order to curb the cost of law school education and to strengthen the position of law school graduates in the market, a group of ten law schools meet to coordinate on efforts to contain costs and to help their graduates in the job search. The ten law schools form a Law School Residency Program through which an administrative body (representing the ten law schools) provide short to long term employment opportunities for graduates. The Program coordinates with potential legal employers on identifying job opportunities and matches students with employers. In addition, the Program replaces the function of law school placement offices thereby reducing costs within the individual law schools. Furthermore, as part of the Program, the law schools attempt to contain expenditures that are deemed unnecessary such as promotional materials and to determine ways to reduce competition with respect to tuition so as to improve competition with respect to quality of legal education.

216. The Program is an example of

(A) a vertical restraint.

(B) a monopolistic entity.

(C) an oligopolistic entity.

(D) a horizontal agreement.

217. If the Program is challenged under the Sherman Act,

(A) it will be immune from a Section One claim since it is a single entity.

(B) it will be subject to a Section Two claim that would require a showing of market power.

(C) it will be subject to a Section One claim because the agreement with employers is a vertical restraint.

(D) it will be subject to a Section Two claim since the law schools are leveraging their position in providing education into a market for recruitment, a per se violation.

218. Suppose in its agreement with potential employers, the Program requires the hiring firm to retain the employee for a fixed period of time and at a certain salary. Which of the following is the most accurate statement based on these facts?

(A) Both the requirement of fixed retention period and the salary are subject to per se analysis under Section One of the Sherman Act.

(B) The fixed retention period is likely to be an ancillary restraint while the salary component is subject to per se analysis.

(C) Both the fixed retention period and the salary would be subject to rule of reason analysis.

(D) The fixed retention period is a per se restriction and the salary term is subject to the rule of reason.

219. If the Program is challenged under antitrust laws, the ten law schools intend to raise the Noerr-Pennington doctrine. This doctrine

(A) will immunize the law schools since they are regulated by the ABA and other entities.

(B) will not immunize the conduct since it is private behavior.

(C) will immunize since there are efficiencies in the venture.

PRACTICE FINAL EXAM

(D) will not immunize since there is no objective basis for entering into the agreement.

220. Suppose one of the potential employees refuses to work with the Program. The ten law schools do not include the potential employee in any of its recruitment efforts and dissuade students from interviewing with the law firm. Such conduct by the law schools

(A) is subject to the rule of reason since it is ancillary to the goals of the Program.

(B) is subject to the rule of reason since it is a vertical agreement.

(C) is subject to per se treatment as a refusal to deal.

(D) is subject to per se treatment as an exclusive dealership.

SHORT ANSWER QUESTIONS: Please write a one paragraph response of about five to ten sentences to each of the following.

221. Briefly discuss the arguments for and against the following statement: Antitrust law should be largely deferential to vertical agreements and focus more on horizontal ones.

ANSWER:

222. Briefly discuss the arguments for and against the following statement: Antitrust law should look closely at monopolies even if there is no monopolistic conduct.

ANSWER:

ANSWERS

1. This question is testing your understanding of the policies and history behind the antitrust laws. See United States v. Joint Traffic Association, 171 U.S. 505 (1898), for a good summary of background. **(A) is incorrect** because U.S. states had unfair competition law before the Sherman Act. Furthermore, some states had laws that limited trusts and other business forms that could lead to monopolies. In addition, there were federal laws that regulated markets and commerce, such as the railroads. **(B) is the correct answer** because English common law did serve as a model for United States antitrust laws, and courts looked to English precedents in developing U.S. antitrust law. **(C) is incorrect** because there are criminal and civil remedies in the Sherman Act. **(D) is incorrect** because the initial goal of the Sherman Act was to reduce market concentration. Maximization of wealth is a goal associated with the law and economics school and did not become as central to antitrust law until the 1970s. The initial goal was to reduce market concentration and prevent monopolies, particularly by promoting small businesses. Reducing market concentration, however, could have the unintended consequence of reducing wealth.

2. This question is testing your understanding of antitrust policies and the debate over the goals of antitrust law. **(A) is incorrect** because the goal is to promote competition, not protect firms. The word exclusively is a clue that the answer might be too broad or not completely accurate. **(B) is incorrect** because market access is a goal of antitrust law particularly through reducing barriers to entry. Arguably, reducing entry would be inconsistent with economic efficiency in many situations. So this choice is too broad and not completely accurate. **(C) is incorrect** because antitrust is concerned with both static and dynamic factors. Markets are meant to be competitive at one point in time, but also competitive over time. **(D) is the correct answer** because it is the least inaccurate. It states a number of goals of the antitrust laws and connects them to particular results such as gains among consumers and firms.

3. This question tests your knowledge of the history of antitrust law and its enforcement. **(A) is incorrect** because courts had great discretion in the early years of the Sherman Act. Some viewed the courts as being too activists, often applying antitrust laws in favor of big business. As a result, Congress responded with the Federal Trade Commission Act and the Clayton Act in 1914, twenty-four years after the passage of the Sherman Act. **(B) is incorrect** because the Department brought several suits challenging anticompetitive practices in the railroad and oil & gas industries, for example. **(C) is the correct answer** because it states how courts did move towards per se rules, striking down even reasonable restrictions on trade that benefitted competition and consumers. **(D) is incorrect** because courts sometimes struck down monopolies even if they were the result of skill or good fortune.

4. The question tests your understanding of the legislative history behind the Sherman Act. **(A) is the correct answer** because English common law on restraint of trade was one source

for the enactment of the Sherman Act. **(B) is incorrect** because the Sherman Act did not abrogate the common law, but adopted it. **(C) is incorrect** because the Sherman Act adopted the common law, not the statute. **(D) is incorrect** because the Sherman Act was aimed at dismantling large companies, not protecting them.

5. This question tests your knowledge about the background history to U.S. antitrust law. **(A) is incorrect** because a covenant not to compete was subject to a standard of reasonableness in some situations such as the sale of a business or the dissolution of a partnership. **(B) is the correct answer**. If the seller of a business could compete with buyer after the sale, then the buyer would have less incentive to buy in the first place. A restraint on competition by the seller, based for example on geography, duration, or industry, would be a reasonable means to protect the buyer and the deal. **(C) is incorrect** because an ancillary restraint was subject to a reasonableness standard. An ancillary restraint is one that is subsidiary to the main purpose of a transaction. It is a side deal. **(D) is incorrect** because sometimes a covenant was per se illegal. However, the dissolution of a partnership was not a situation in which the restraint was per illegal. Instead, a restraint on competition would be reasonable in that case.

6. This question tests your knowledge of terminology. **(A) is incorrect** because an ancillary restraint is subject to a reasonableness standard. An ancillary restraint is a side deal, and restraints in side deals were treated differently from agreements whose primary purpose was to restrain trade. **(B) is the correct answer** because it correctly states the definition of an ancillary restraint. **(C) is incorrect** because an ancillary restraint was subject to a reasonableness standard under both bodies of law. **(D) is incorrect** because the standard was one of reasonableness and so the answer is imprecise.

7. This question tests your knowledge of terminology and concepts. **(A) is incorrect** because distributional and political goals mattered as well for antitrust laws. See Question 1, above. **(B) is the correct answer** because it states a correct definition of economic efficiency. If resources can be reallocated so as to make parties better off without hurting anyone else, the resources are not allocated efficiently. However, if consumers and producers are benefitted in the best possible way so that the gains from trade, or surplus, is maximized, the allocation is efficient. **(C) is incorrect** because exchange may not lead to efficiency if there are externalities or information asymmetries. **(D) is incorrect** because sometimes agreements serve to enhance efficiency such as a covenant not to compete in the sale of a business.

8. This question tests your knowledge about the differences between Sections One and Two of the Sherman Act. **(A) is incorrect** because monopolization occurs through the action of one entity. **(B) is incorrect** because agreements among buyers are actionable as an illegal monopsony or buyer collusion. **(C) is the correct answer** because it accurately states the basic difference between Sections One and Two of the Sherman Act. **(D) is incorrect** because the second part about agreement among small firms is inaccurate. Agreements even among small firms can be illegal under the Sherman Act.

9. This question tests your knowledge of the background history of the Sherman Act and can be reviewed with Question 3. **(A) is incorrect** because the Sherman Act was used against labor unions, which were viewed as a type of restraint of trade. **(B) is incorrect** because intellectual property sometimes immunized a firm from antitrust scrutiny. **(C) is the correct answer** because courts did read the Sherman Act strictly to make illegal many agreements

among competitors even if the agreement was reasonable. **(D) is incorrect** because the law tracked English common law both with respect to the sale of a business and to the dissolution of partnerships.

10. This question tests your knowledge of the application of the Sherman Act in its early years and currently. **(A) is incorrect** because in the early years interpretation was largely through judicial opinions and there was little or no regulations or guidelines from agencies. **(B) is the correct answer** because the two agencies have converged in their treatment of mergers and operate under similar guidelines. **(C) is incorrect** because it is a correct statement about the source of FTC power. **(D) is incorrect** because the DOJ does have broad sub poena powers through its ability to institute civil investigative demands.

11. The Sherman Act was enacted to deal with market concentration through the expansion of firms by acquisition and merger. The concern was that such large firms would hurt society through higher prices and through undue influence on politics. Instead of engaging in healthy competition, corporations were seen as colluding with each other and obtaining market power. Over time, antitrust laws developed to deal with anticompetitive contractual practices and price discrimination that benefitted large retail firms at the expense of smaller ones. More recently, antitrust law has been driven by concerns with economic harms to consumers as measured by losses in economic efficiency. Thus turn in antitrust law suggests that some market concentration may be appropriate to stimulate economic growth and innovation. In addition, firms might benefit from cooperating, rather than competing, in order to engage in research and development.

12. Antitrust laws are enforced either through civil litigation that can be initiated by a private company injured by anticompetitive conduct or by a governmental entity. The governmental entity can include the Department of Justice, the Federal Trade Commission, or state attorneys general. The Department of Justice can bring criminal proceedings against the defendant. While the legal standards for a violation are the same for both a private and a governmental plaintiff, there are important differences. The private plaintiff must show antitrust standing and can obtain treble damages. The governmental plaintiff usually seeks an injunction and has the power of civil investigative demand to sub poena the antitrust defendant to obtain information through discovery.

13. This question tests your understanding of markets under economic theory. A perfectly competitive market is one in which there are many firms and consumers, each acting as a price taker, each having perfect and complete information, each acting rationally, and into which entry is unconstrained. **(A) is incorrect** because in a perfectly competitive market entry is unconstrained, meaning that there are no barriers to entry like intellectual property. **(B) is the correct answer** because in a perfectly competitive market no individual firm or consumer can control the price and so each market actor takes the price as given. **(C) is incorrect** because, in the long run, competition reduces profits to a normal level. **(D) is incorrect** because consumers pay a uniform price, and price discrimination is not possible.

14. This question tests your understanding of monopoly under economic theory. A monopoly market is one in which there is one seller and many buyers. The one seller can set the market price but is constrained by the market demand for the product. **(A) is incorrect** because there is only one dominant firm in a monopoly. **(B) is incorrect** because a monopolist cannot set both quantity and price because it is constrained by the market demand curve. **(C) is the correct answer** because it captures the elements of a monopoly. **(D) is incorrect** because a monopoly can result in other ways than from the integration of firms, for example, through the exit of firms.

15. This question tests your understanding of oligopoly under economic theory. An oligopoly is a market in which there are a few firms and many sellers. In an oligopoly, firms act strategically based on their beliefs about how other firms would act in serving the market. **(A) is the correct answer** because an oligopoly is a market with a few firms because entry of new firms is difficult. **(B) is incorrect** because it accurately describes one possibility in an oligopoly. **(C) is incorrect** because firms in an oligopoly do engage in a form of competition. **(D) is incorrect** because this description is accurate.

16. This question tests your knowledge of elasticity under economic theory. Elasticity measures the percentage change in one variable predicted when one other variable changes, holding everything else constant. Price elasticity measures the percentage change in quantity demanded when price changes, holding everything else constant. **(A) is incorrect** because income is held fix to calculate price elasticity. **(B) is incorrect** because price is the only variable that changes. **(C) is incorrect** because price is the only variable that changes. **(D) is the correct answer** because it is the most correct in stating the definition. Implicit in the statement is that other variables are not changing.

17. This question tests your understanding of the elasticity concept. (A) is a true statement as is (B). (A) is true because an elasticity close to zero means that quantity demanded does not change very much when price changes. The demand is sensitive to variables other than price. For example, certain necessities might not be sensitive to price. A purchaser might not

change monthly purchases of a product if the price changes. (B) is also accurate because if there are lots of substitutes, a purchaser can switch to other products if the price of a good rises. So **the correct choice is (D)**.

18.   This question again tests your understanding of elasticity, this time on the supply side. Elasticity of supply measures how market supply changes as price changes. Market supply adjusts by new firms entering and each firm adjusting supply in response to the price change, holding everything else constant. **(A) is incorrect** because this condition affects demand elasticity not supply. **(B) is the correct answer** because entry of new firms will affect the quantity supplied in the market. **(C) is incorrect** because technologies are held fixed to calculate elasticity. **(D) is incorrect** because firms are assumed to take price as given.

19.   This question tests your understanding of the Lerner Index, which is used to measure market concentration. The Lerner Index aggregates information about market shares and elasticity of demand and supply. **(A) is incorrect** because market share is only one factor in calculating the index. **(B) is incorrect** because number of firms is only one factor in calculating the index. **(C) is the correct answer** since the Index aggregates all of these factors. **(D) is incorrect** because a zero measure of the index is consistent with perfect competition.

20.   This question tests your knowledge about how a monopoly market operates under economic theory. A monopolist maximizing profits will set the price based on the demand curve and its cost structure. It will sell where the extra revenue from a sale (marginal revenue) will equal the extra cost of production (marginal cost). The prediction is that the price will be a mark-up of marginal cost where the mark-up will be based on elasticity of demand. **(A) is incorrect** because a monopolist will charge a mark-up on marginal cost. **(B) is incorrect** because a monopolist will operate on the elastic portion of the market demand curve. **(C) is the correct answer** for the reasons stated earlier in this paragraph. **(D) is incorrect** because a profit maximizing firm will base its decision on the market demand curve, not on the reactions of other firms.

21.   This question tests your knowledge of the term market power. Market power refers to the ability of a firm (or consumer) to affect variables in a market place, such as price, quantity, or number of firms. **(D) is the correct answer** because A, B, and C are each true.

22.   This question tests your knowledge of the Lerner Index, tested question 19. Remember the Lerner Index aggregates information about market share and elasticities. **(A) is incorrect** because market power captures the ability of a firm to shape the market in the future. Current market share may not measure this power. **(B) is the correct answer** because a high market share with low elasticities of demand and supply suggest that consumers may not respond to price changes by switching to other products and that new firms cannot readily the market. **(C) is incorrect** because supply elasticity also matters. **(D) is incorrect** for the same reason as A.

23.   This question tests your understanding of the limitations with the Lerner Index. **(A) is incorrect** because it describes a consequence of market power, not an indicator. **(B) is the correct answer** because one has to know what the relevant market is in order to measure market share and elasticities. **(C) is incorrect** because it ignores the problem of market

definition. **(D) is incorrect** because the numbers are not always manipulable.

24. This question tests your understanding of market definition. Before measure concepts like the Lerner Index, one has to know what the relevant market is. Market definition requires understanding the relevant product or service, the relevant geography, and the relevant time frame. One approach to determining market definition is to use cross price elasticity of demand. Put simply, under this approach, one starts with a narrow definition of a product or service and then looks to see how demand for that narrow category would be affected by a change in price for a related product or service. If demand for the narrow good goes up when the price falls, then the case can be made that two products or services are in the same market. **(A), (B), and (C) are each incorrect** because each is an accurate statement. **(D) is the correct answer** because a high cross price elasticity of demand is consistent with market power since a monopolist will price on the elastic portion of the market demand curve where demand is sensitive to price.

25. This question tests your understanding of market definition. See question 24 for more details. **(A) is the correct answer** because each concept does not presume that the market has been defined. **(B) is incorrect** because the Lerner Index assumes we have defined the market. **(C) and (D) are incorrect** because market share assumes market definition.

26. This question tests your knowledge of oligopoly and cartels, which is an agreement among firms. **(A) is incorrect** because a cartel cannot arise in a monopoly market where there is only one firm. **(B) is incorrect** since a cartel can keep out new firms. **(C) is the correct answer** for the same reason that **(D) is incorrect**. If the firms can see what other firms do, the cartel may tend to be stable as firms can punish a firm that tries to break the cartel.

27. This question tests your understanding of the concept of price discrimination, which is examined more thoroughly in the last chapter of this book. Price discrimination means that a firm charges different prices to different consumers for the same product or service during the same period of time. **(A) is incorrect** because price discrimination could not occur in a perfectly competitive market since all firms take the market price as given. **(B) is the correct answer** because price discrimination can allow access to a product or service that might be available if the firm had to charge everyone the same price. **(C) is incorrect** because the exact opposite of what is stated is true. **(D) is incorrect** because consumers can be made better off through price discrimination if they otherwise would not be able to purchase the good at all.

28. Economic theory provides an analytic framework for understanding how competition and markets operate. This framework includes an explanation of concepts such as cost, demand, supply, and market equilibrium. Specifically, economic theory introduces the concept of perfect price competition which describes how rational consumers and firms respond to price under conditions of symmetric and complete information and no barriers to entry or exit. Economic theory also addresses other market structures such as monopoly, oligopoly, and monopolistic competition. Finally, economic theory provides the concept of efficiency, sometimes defines as wealth maximization, to assess when competition is operating effectively and when competition needs to be corrected through government intervention such as antitrust law.

29. Elasticity measures the percent change in one variable when another variable changes by

one percent, holding everything else fixed. The key use of the elasticity concept is in the price elasticity of demand which measures the percent change in quantity demanded when price changes by one percent. There are two types of price elasticity of demand. Own price elasticity of demand measures how quantity demand changes when the price of the good changes by one percent. Cross price elasticity of demand measures how quantity demand changes when the price of another good changes by one percent. Own price elasticity is used to gauge how competitive a market is and how readily consumers can respond to a price change. Cross price elasticity of demand is used for the purposes of market definition. A negative cross price elasticity means goods are complements and are in the same market. A positive cross price elasticity means goods are substitutes and are in different markets.

30.   This question tests your understanding of antitrust standing. **(A) is incorrect** because indirect purchasers in general cannot bring a suit, only direct purchasers. **(B) is the correct answer** because the Clayton Act states this as the basis for determining who can bring an antitrust suit. **(C) is incorrect** because injunctions are available. **(D) is incorrect** because only economic injury is recoverable.

31.   This question tests your understanding of the concept of antitrust injury, a requirement in addition to standing for a court to hear an antitrust claim. Antitrust laws remedy harms to competition, not to individual competitors, firms, or consumers. **(A) is incorrect** because increased competition is not an injury. **(B) is incorrect** because the loss of profits is an individual loss, not an injury to competition. **(C) is incorrect** because lawsuits are sometimes immune from antitrust scrutiny under the Noerr-Pennington doctrine. **(D) is the correct answer** because the price fixing scheme is an injury to the competitive process and that injury is the basis for the price increase suffered by the direct purchaser.

32.   This question tests your understanding of the indirect purchaser rule, which states that only a direct purchaser has standing to bring an antitrust suit with some exceptions. **(A) is incorrect** because the party is a nonconspirator. Only if two entities are conspirators can the indirect purchaser have standing in this case. **(B) is incorrect** because the retailer and manufacturer are separate entities. If they were the same entity (for example, a parent and subsidiary company), then the indirect purchaser can sue, **(C) is incorrect** because the indirect purchaser may not have standing even if damages are the remedy. **(D) is the correct answer** and states the main exception to the indirect purchaser rule.

33.   This question tests your knowledge of when the U.S. antitrust laws can be applied to acts outside the U.S. **(A) is incorrect** because the Clayton Act does not apply extraterritorially. **(B) is incorrect** because the statement is accurate. **(C) is the correct answer** because the Clayton Act claim would not survive. **(D) is incorrect** because lack of subject matter would be a basis for dismissing the suit.

34.   This question tests your knowledge of the Noerr-Pennington Doctrine, which states that political lobbying even for economic advantage by hurting a competitor does not provide the basis for an antitrust claim. **(A) is incorrect** because the doctrine immunizes the acts described. **(B) is the correct answer** because it accurately states the doctrine. **(C) is incorrect** because lobbying in general is immunized from review. **(D) is incorrect** because such action is not always immune.

35.   This question tests your knowledge of the concept of natural monopoly. A natural monopoly is one that arises because of the nature of production or because of legislation, either of which might make it difficult for new firms to enter a market. **(A) is incorrect** because there is no such immunity for a natural monopoly. **(B) is the correct answer** because a natural

monopoly, such as telephone or utilities, might be subject to regulation and the regulation may create an immunity. **(C) is incorrect** because there can be bases for regulation even if the market is contestable. A contestable market is one where there is potential entry which acts as effective competition for the natural monopolist. Airlines are considered an example of contestable markets. But contestability does not rule out the need for regulation. **(D) is incorrect** because there is no such rule.

36.   This question tests your understanding about the relationship between economic regulation and antitrust. Read each answer Choice (C)arefully because each makes an accurate statement. **(A), (B), and (C) are each accurate, and therefore incorrect. (D) is the correct answer.**

37.   This question tests your understanding of antitrust immunity. **(B) is the correct answer** because the McCarren-Ferguson Act expressly exempts the insurance industry from the antitrust laws. This exemption was an issue during the health care reform debates in 2009-2010. There is no express immunity for **(A), (C), or (D), making them all incorrect choices.**

38.   This question tests your knowledge of the state action doctrine, which immunizes a state government from antitrust liability even if it enacts legislation that is anticompetitive. The doctrine recognizes state sovereignty in regulating the economy. **(A) is incorrect** because the state action doctrine frees the state from liability. **(B) is incorrect** because wineries would be immune as well since they are acting in compliance with state law. **(C) is the correct answer** because the state would be immunized from liability. **(D) is incorrect** because it states the rule for municipal or agency immunity, not state.

39.   This question tests your understanding of the state action doctrine as applied to local governments. You should review the answer here in conjunction with Question 38, especially answer choice (D). **(A) is incorrect** because immunity is conditional for an agency. **(B) is incorrect** because the agency has some immunity. **(C) is the correct answer** because it states the rule for when local government entities have immunity. **(D) is incorrect** because the agency has some immunity as described in answer (C).

40.   This question tests your understanding of the Civil Investigative Demand, which gives the DoJ broad sub poena powers in engage in antitrust investigations. **(A) is incorrect** because it is the Department of Justice that has the power. **(B) is the correct answer** because it correctly defines the term. **(C) is incorrect** because the Department has the power. **(D) is incorrect** because private parties do not have this power.

41.   This question tests your knowledge of the Clayton Act. **(A) is incorrect** because it is only partly true. Other provisions also govern such as the Sherman Act. **(B) is incorrect** because not only private parties are allowed to sue. **(C) is the correct answer** because it states accurately who can sue and the standard for liability. **(D) is incorrect** because it also applies to the Department of Justice.

42.   This question tests your knowledge of how anticompetitive litigation can be a basis for an antitrust claim. The basic rule is one of the sham exception to immunity from liability for suing a competitor. In general, one competitor can sue another without fear of antitrust

liability unless the lawsuit was a sham, intended to harass or otherwise harm the competitor. Antitrust liability arises if there was no objective or subjective basis for bringing the lawsuit. **(A) is incorrect** because it ignores the immunity for the lawsuit. **(B) is incorrect** because any immunity is not absolute. **(C) is the correct answer** because it states the objective and subjective requirements for showing a sham. **(D) is incorrect** because the state action doctrine is irrelevant.

43. This question tests your knowledge about the relationship between federal antitrust law and state law. **(A) is incorrect** because the AG has to meet certain requirements. **(B) is incorrect** because there is no such rule. **(C) is incorrect** since the AG can bring a concurrent suit. **(D) is the correct answer** since the state AG has to meet the same requirements as a private plaintiff.

44. This question tests your knowledge of when the Federal Government can be sued for antitrust violations. It asks whether there is a federal equivalent of the state action doctrine, tested in Questions 38 and 39. **(A) is incorrect** because there is no such blanket immunity. **(B) is the correct answer** because it states the law correctly. **(C) is incorrect** because there is no such general rule. **(D) is incorrect** because there is no such rule.

45. Antitrust immunity removes certain individuals or acts from antitrust liability for policy reasons. One example of antitrust immunity is the State Action Doctrine, which holds that a state government is not liable for enacting legislation that has anticompetitive effects. An example would be state legislation that protects the agricultural industry within the state from competition. The purpose behind the State Action Doctrine is to allow states to engage in legislative experimentation and to promote local economies. The State Action Doctrine also applies to municipal entities and state agencies, which are immunized if the state has active supervision over the entity or agency and the action by the entity or the agency comes from a clearly articulated policy of the state.

46. The Noerr-Pennington Doctrine is a type of antitrust immunity that immunizes certain conduct by parties that might otherwise be subject to antitrust liability. Specifically, the Doctrine immunizes activities by individuals to lobby the legislature or to pursue administrative proceedings that might have anticompetitive effect. For example, if a company lobbies for stricter regulation that might hurt competitors or seeks a zoning ordinance that might limit entry of new businesses, such activities are immunized from antitrust law. The policy behind this immunity is to separate political activity from commercial activity , including only the second under antitrust laws.

47. This question tests your understanding of the difference between rule of reason and per se treatment of agreements. In general, if an agreement is subject to the rule of reason, courts will examine the pro-competitive benefits and anti-competitive effects of the agreements. Under per se treatment, the agreement is deemed illegal on its face. **(A) is incorrect** because some horizontal restraints are subject to the rule of reason. For example, horizontal agreements not involving price fixing or territorial arrangements, vertical agreements, and agreements among professionals are often judged under the rule of reason. *See, e.g.*, FTC v. Indiana Federation of Dentists, 476 U.S. 447 (1986) (agreement among dentists not to release x-rays to insurance companies judged under rule of reason). **(B) is incorrect** because horizontal territorial restrictions are per se illegal. *See* United States v. Socony-Vacuum Oil Company, 310 U.S. 150 (1940). **(C) is the correct answer** because it states an accurate definition of the rule of reason. **(D) is incorrect** because it ignores the rule of reason.

48. This question tests your knowledge of the term per se rule or per se analysis. **(A) is incorrect** because per se means illegal without evidence of harmful effects, which are presumed from the conduct. **(B) is the correct answer** because it states the correct definition of illegality without regard to effects. Market power is not relevant for per se analysis. See Socony-Vacuum, cited in Question 47. **(C) is incorrect** because market power is irrelevant for the per se rule, except in the case of tying. See materials in Chapter 7. **(D) is incorrect** because this answer choice vaguely states the rule for quick look rule of reason, not per se analysis. *See* National Athletic Association v. University of Oklahoma, 468 U.S. 85 (1984) (putting forth quick look rule of reason).

49. This question tests your understanding of the term quick look rule of reason. See discussion with respect to answer Choice (D) in Question 48. Under the quick look, agencies or courts create a presumption of anticompetitive harm with the burden shifting to the defendant to show a justification. After California Dental v. FTC, 526 U.S. 756 (1999), quick look has become less relevant. **(A) is the correct answer** because it states the correct definition. **(B) is incorrect** because there is no such presumption. **(C) is incorrect** because it misstates the rule. **(D) is incorrect** because the standard of review and scrutiny is not at issue.

50. This question tests your knowledge about price fixing. Keep in mind there are two kinds: vertical and horizontal. This chapter covers horizontal agreements and so the second type of price fixing is at issue. Price fixing among competitors is per se illegal even if the firms acting in concert have no market power. See Question 48 above. **(A) is incorrect** because it states the rule of reason. **(B) is incorrect** because market division is not the issue. **(C) is the correct answer**; see Socony-Vacuum cited above in Question 48. **(D) is incorrect** because it vaguely states the rule for predatory pricing, a different claim that would arise under Section Two of the Sherman Act.

51.   This question tests your knowledge of cartels, an agreement among competitors in an industry to control price or some other aspect of the market. Cartels must police itself to insure members do not cheat on the cartel agreement. Because of the possibility of cheating, cartels are sometimes seen as unstable arrangements that might fall apart without legal intervention. The concern for the law is a strong cartel which can go undetected, creating the appearance of competition when in fact there is none. **(A) is incorrect** because there is no such rule. **(B) is the correct answer** because if members cannot monitor each other, the cartel can fall apart. **(C) is incorrect** because product heterogeneity would make it more difficult to monitor the cartel and therefore make it weaker. **(D) is incorrect** because more firms makes the cartel more unstable.

52.   This question tests your knowledge of cartels and the per se rule against price fixing. If an agreement is indirectly fixing price, it will be found to be per se illegal. See Socony-Vacuum, cited in Question 48, which involved restrictions in quantity like this one. **(A), (B), and (C) are each inaccurate** because each misstates the rule for per se illegality of price fixing. **(D) is the correct answer** because it explains that restrictions on quantity are a way to raise price.

53.   This question tests your knowledge of the ancillary restraint doctrine. As discussed in Chapter One, the ancillary restraint doctrine has roots in English common law and states that a restraint on trade is not illegal if it is ancillary to a main agreement and reasonable. *See* Addyston Pipe & Steel v. United States, 85 F. 271 (6th Cir. 1898). **(A) is incorrect** because it misstates the rule. An ancillary restraint is legal if it is reasonable. **(B) is incorrect** because ancillary restraints are subject to the rule of reason. **(C) is the correct answer** because it states the rule of reason treatment of ancillary restraints. **(D) is incorrect** because reasonableness, not market power, is the basis for liability.

54.   This question tests your knowledge of the quick look rule of reason and its relationship to other rules in antitrust law. See Question 49. **(A) is the correct answer** because under quick look there is a presumption of anticompetitive effects. **(B) is incorrect** because market power is not relevant. **(C) is incorrect** because the standard applies to agreements other than those that deal with price. **(D) is incorrect** because the standard applies to other agreements as well.

55.   This question tests your understanding of agreements among members of a professional association. See Question 47 above. On the issue of agreements not to compete at all, see National Society of Professional Engineers v. United States, 435 U.S. 679 (1978). **(A) is incorrect** because the agreement is in a per se category. **(B) is incorrect** because firms cannot agree not to compete. **(C) is the correct answer** since competition can occur based on quality as well as price and other variables. **(D) is incorrect** because the agreement is in a per se category.

56.   This question tests your knowledge of price fixing and cartels. The question specifically asks about crisis cartels, which were held to be an exception to the per se rule against horizontal price fixing in Appalachian Coals, Inc. v. United States, 288 U.S. 344 (1938). **(A) is incorrect** because market power is irrelevant. **(B) is the correct answer** because it describes accurately the concept of crisis cartels. **(C) is incorrect** because there is no such procedure for joint review. **(D) is incorrect** because there is no such rule.

57. This question tests your understanding of agreements among professionals. See Question 55 for more details. **(A) is incorrect** because there is no such per se legal category. **(B) is incorrect** because some agreements may be subject to per se treatment if they deal with price or territorial divisions. **(C) is the correct answer** because price restrictions will make the agreement fall into the per se category. **(D) is incorrect** because there is no such rule.

58. This question tests your knowledge of antitrust treatment of agreements in the professional context, in this case professional schools. *See* Massachusetts School of Law v. ABA, 142 F.3d 26 (1st Cir. 1998). **(A) is incorrect** because there is no per se legal category. **(B) is the correct answer** because if there is no agreement as to price or to divisions of territory, there is no basis for a per se rule. Under the rule of reason, there would be pro-competitive justifications. **(C) is incorrect** because market power is not a requirement. **(D) is incorrect** because price sharing may not lead to price fixing.

59. This question tests your knowledge of territorial division among competitors. *See* Palmer v. BRG of Georgia, Inc., 498 U.S. 46 (1990). **(A) is incorrect** because market power is not relevant. **(B) is the correct answer** because a horizontal territorial division is subject to the per se rule. **(C) is incorrect** because a territorial restriction like this one is per se illegal. **(D) is incorrect** because market power is not relevant.

60. This question tests your knowledge of market power in the context of claims under Section One of the Sherman Act. In general, Section One is aimed at agreements among competitors, who as a general matter should engage in competition not in cooperation, except in some situations. Market power is irrelevant for Section One claims in general because the concern is with preserving the competitive process. However, if there is market power among the parties to the agreement, then the anticompetitive effects may outweigh the procompetitive benefits under the rule of reason. **(A) is incorrect** because market power may be relevant to infer anticompetitive effects for a rule of reason analysis. **(B) is incorrect** because there is no such rule. **(C) is the correct answer** because market power might be relevant for identifying anticompetitive effects. **(D) is incorrect** because it states vaguely a rule under Section Two of the Sherman Act.

61. This question tests your understanding of agreements among competitors to set a maximum price, in other words a price ceiling. Logically, one might think that a price ceiling is not harmful since it tends to keep prices low. As we will see in Chapter Five, that is the logic for vertical agreements. But that is not the rule for horizontal agreements. Competitors are expected to compete on price and so a maximum price is treated like minimum prices, or a price floor. *See* Albrecht v. Herald Co., 390 U.S. 145 (1968). **(A) is the correct answer** because it states that rule that agreement to either minimum or maximum prices is per se illegal. **(B) is incorrect** because the agreement is one to fix price, subject to per se analysis. **(C) is incorrect** because there is no per se legal category. **(D) is incorrect** because there is no such rule.

62. This question tests your understanding of the concept of joint venture, an agreement among competitors to engage in research and development or other activities that enhance the market. *See* Texaco v. Dagher, 547 U.S. 1 (2006), which deals with a joint venture among oil companies. The issue is whether a joint venture is a single entity, which cannot be a basis for liability under Section One of the Sherman Act. **(A) is incorrect** because there is no per se legal category. **(B) is incorrect** because some joint ventures might be subject to the per se

rule, for example, if they engage in price fixing. **(C) is incorrect** because there is no such rule. **(D) is the correct answer** because under Texaco, a joint venture is considered one entity. Compare with American Needle v. NFL, 130 S. Ct. 2201 (2010) in which the Court held that the creation of a corporation by members of the NFL to engage in licensing was not a single entity because the licensors maintained separate identities.

63.   This question tests your understanding of the National Cooperative Research Act, legislation that deals with research and development joint ventures. **(A) is incorrect** because the Act has some requirements for the rule of reason to apply such as registration and reporting and the requirement that the venture deals in research and development and product development. **(B) is the correct answer** because it states the requirements for rule of reason treatment. **(C) is incorrect** because the Act removes treble damages. **(D) is incorrect** because the Act imposes the rule of reason, not the quick look.

64.   This question tests your understanding of a group boycott, or an agreement among competitors to not deal with another competitor, a supplier, or a buyer. Group boycotts may be part of a larger agreement to set price or exclude entry. A group boycott is also known as a concerted refusal to deal. *See* Fashion Originators Guild v. FTC, 312 U.S. 457 (1941); Klor's, Inc. v. Broadway Hale Stores, Inc., 359 U.S. 207 (1959). **(A), (B), and (C) are each correct, making them incorrect choices**; therefore, **(D) is the correct answer**. Per se versus rule of reason depends on whether the refusal to deal is part of a broader agreement to fix prices or restrict territories, either of which would give rise to per se treatment.

65.   This question tests your knowledge of concerted refusals to deal, another name for a group boycott. See Question 64. **(A) is incorrect** because there is no such rule for professional associations. **(B) is the correct answer** because treatment of groups boycotts rests on whether it is part of a broader illegal agreement. **(C) is incorrect** because group boycotts fall into a per se illegal category. **(D) is incorrect** because there is no such rule.

66.   This question tests your knowledge of market divisions among competitors, a type of horizontal agreement. See Question 59. **(A) is the correct answer** because it describes the three principal ways in which a market can be divided. **(B) is incorrect** because such divisions are subject to per analysis. **(C) is incorrect** because there is no such rule. **(D) is incorrect** because there is no such rule.

67.   This question tests your understanding of how a price fixing agreement can be proven. **(A) is incorrect** because the agreement need not be express and could be tacit. **(B) is the correct answer** because it shows the essential element which is an agreement and also points out that the agreement can be either explicit or tacit. **(C) is incorrect** because market power is not required. **(D) is incorrect** because price fixing is subject to a per se rule.

68.   This question tests your knowledge of how price fixing can be established through evidence of a tacit agreement. Parallel conduct among competitors can be evidence of an implicit agreement. **(A) and (D) are incorrect** because an express agreement is not required. **(B) is incorrect** because market power is not required. **(C) is the correct answer** because it identifies a set of acts that would strongly suggest a tacit agreement to set price. *See* Interstate Circuit v. United States, 306 U.S. 208 (1939).

69.   This questions tests your knowledge of conscious parallelism. *See* Compliant, In re Ethyl

Corp., CCH Trade Reg. Reporter 21, 570 (1979). A and B are both true. **(C)** **is the correct answer**.

70. A Section One violation requires two or more firms acting in concert. If there is only firm, there is not Section One claim, but there might be a Section Two claim. When are there two or more firms? The answer choices present the relevant scenarios. *See* Copperweld Corp. v. Independence Tube Corp., 467 U.S. 752 (1984); Poller v. CBS, Inc., 368 U.S. 464 (1962). **(A) is incorrect** because the corporation and wholly owned subsidiary are one entity. **(B) is incorrect** because the joint venture in this scenario would be one entity. See Question 62. **(C) is the correct answer** because members of a trade association are considered independent entities. **(D) is incorrect** because corporation and its agents are one entity since an agent acts on behalf of the corporation.

71. This question asks about the intent requirement for criminal liability under the Sherman Act. *See* United States v. U.S. Gypsum Co., 438 U.S. 422 (1978). **(A) is incorrect** because general intent can be sufficient. **(B) is incorrect** because per se analysis can apply to criminal liability. **(C) is incorrect** because some showing of intent is required. **(D) is the correct answer** since either level of intent is sufficient and actual anticompetitive effects can show that there was general intent to violate the antitrust laws.

72. A horizontal agreement is one among competitors who operate at the same level of the distribution chain. An agreement among manufacturers or among retailers would be a horizontal agreement while one between a manufacture and a retailer would be a vertical agreement. Although some scholars criticize the term, it is standard in antitrust law. The view is that firms operating at the same level of the distribution chain have little reason for agreement and should operate competitively at arm's length. Therefore, horizontal agreements are suspect under antitrust law. At the same time, agreements among horizontal competitors are necessary for business. For example, one competitor might sell a business to another. In such situations, antitrust laws might lower its level of scrutiny but still look upon such agreements with suspicion.

73. A per se rule states that a particular agreement is illegal on its face under the antitrust laws. Rule of reason applies to all agreements that are not per se and requires a balancing of pro-competitive and anti-competitive consequences of the agreement. An agreement that is per se illegal is one that is without question harmful to competition. One example is a horizontal agreement to set prices. Such an agreement harms competition because it interferes with the price system that is considered the main mechanism through which market competition operates. An agreement such as imposing a standard for the production of a product might have pro-competitive benefits even though the standard might have anti-competitive effects by excluding firms that do not comply. In such situations, the rule of reason would apply.

74. This question tests your knowledge about the difference between vertical restraints and horizontal restraints. **(A), (B), and (D) are each accurate statements, and, therefore, incorrect. (C) is the correct answer** because the Sherman Act and Clayton Act both apply to both horizontal and vertical restraints.

75. This question tests your understanding of the economic effects of a vertical price restraint, which is a restriction placed on a retailer or distributor by a manufacturer on the pricing of a product. Minimum vertical price restrictions serve to limit price competition among retailers who have an incentive to undercut each other to attract customers. The problem with this type of price competition is that it might hurt the manufacturer and the value of the brand. Maximum vertical price restraints are used to limit monopoly power by certain retailers that might have regional monopolies. Both maximum and minimum vertical price restrictions can benefit consumers. See the extensive discussion in Leegin v. PKS, Inc., 127 S. Ct. 2705 (2007). **(A) is incorrect** because such restraints may reduce intrabrand competition while promoting interbrand competition. **(B) is incorrect** because better provision of services would enhance consumer welfare. **(C) is incorrect** because the increased prices might lead to better services for consumers. **(D) is the correct answer** because it reflects the notion that vertical price restrictions can benefit consumers.

76. This question tests your understanding of the economics and policy underlying vertical non-price restrictions. Such restrictions entail a restraint imposed by the manufacturer on retailers with respect to territory of sale, quality control, or other contractual limitations. **(A) is incorrect** because non-price restraints can make it more difficult for new firms to enter. **(B) is incorrect** because non-price restraints might affect competition and market adjustment. **(C) is the correct answer** because non-price restraints are designed to limit competition among retailers so as to improve the brand and help the manufacturer in promoting the product. **(D) is incorrect** because it describes a requirements contract, which is one type of restraint.

77. This question tests your knowledge on horizontal price restrictions and is meant as a review of concepts from Chapter Four to check that you understand the difference between vertical and horizontal restraints. **(A) is the correct answer** because agreements among competitors are in general thought to be harmful because they deprive consumers of the value of competition. **(B), (C) and (D) are incorrect** because each answer confuses vertical with horizontal restraints.

78. This question tests your understanding of dual distributorships, which arise when a manufacturer both directly distributes to consumers and works through independent retailers. *See* Krehl v. Baskin-Robbins Ice Cream Co., 664 F.2d 1348 (9th Cir. 1982). **(A) is the correct answer** because it states the correct definition. **(B) and (C) are inaccurate** because treatment is subject to rule of reason analysis. **(D) is incorrect** because it describes

a group boycott, not a dual distributorship.

79. This question tests your knowledge about the development of rules governing vertical restraints. See Question 68 to review some details. **(A) is incorrect** because the movement has been towards rule of reason treatment. **(B) is the correct answer** because as the Leegin case shows (see Question 68), rule of reason is the approach for all vertical restraints. **(C) is incorrect** because it misstates the rule that vertical restraints, even maximum resale price restraints, are subject to the rule of reason. **(D) is incorrect** because maximum is not always a disguised form of minimum although sometimes this argument is made.

80. This question tests your understanding of the development of the rule on minimum resale price restraints. Question 68 and the Leegin case cited in the answer provide background. For the treatment of consignments as an exception to the old per se rule, see United States v. General Electric, 272 U.S. 476 (1926); Simpson v. Union Oil, 377 U.S. 13 (1964). **(A) is the correct answer** because it states the correct rule on consignment sales from the GE and Simpson cases. **(B) is incorrect** because the restraint used to be subject to a per se rule. **(C) is incorrect** because the rule used to be that patent ownership would be a basis for rule of reason treatment. **(D) is incorrect** because the antitrust treatment is the same whether the retailer or the manufacturer requests the restraint.

81. This question tests your understanding of vertical non-price restraints, such as territorial or product line restrictions. See Leegin in Question 68 for discussion of these types of restraints in comparison with price restraints. See Continental T. V, Inc. v. GTE Sylvania, 433 U.S. 36 (1977) for the current treatment of vertical non-price restraints, which are subject to the rule of reason. **(C) is the correct answer** since the rule on minimum resale price maintenance was one of the last to change. **(A), (B), and (D) are each true statements, and, therefore, incorrect.**

82. This question tests your knowledge about vertical non-price restraints and maximum resale price maintenance. For a discussion of maximum resale price maintenance, see State Oil v. Khan, 522 U.S. 3 (1997), overruling per se rule against maximum resale price maintenance and establishing rule o reason treatment. **(A) is incorrect** because the rationale is true about maximum and not minimum prices. **(B) is incorrect** because the rationale stated apples to minimum not maximum price. **(C) is incorrect** because while entry may be reduced, that is not an explanation for the use of minimum prices. **(D) is the correct answer** because maximum resale price restraints serve to prevent the exercise the potential monopoly power of local retailers. Such monopoly power can arise from the retailer being the sole distributor in a geographic area.

83. This question tests your knowledge about minimum resale price maintenance. See Question 68 and the Leegin case cited in that answer. **(A) is incorrect** because it does not distinguish between interbrand and intrabrand competition. **(B) is incorrect** because the restraint does not necessarily prevent market power. **(C) is the correct answer** because prevention of free riding and cost cutting among retailers are justifications for minimum resale price maintenance. **(D) is incorrect** because it misstates the law.

84. This question tests your understanding of how to show an illegal vertical agreement. See Business Electronics v. Sharp, 485 U.S. 717 (1988), for a discussion of the development of this area of law. Under Sharp, a plaintiff alleging an illegal vertical price restraint has to

show agreement with respect to price or price levels. The Sharp decision built on that in Monsanto v. Spray-Rite Service Corp., 465 U.S. 752 (1984), which held that proof of termination of retailer by a manufacturer would support proof of a vertical agreement. Under United States v. Colgate, 250 U.S. 300 (1919), a refusal by a manufacture to deal with a retailer would not by itself be a basis for proof of an agreement of a vertical restraint. Furthermore, Frey & Sons. v. Cudahy, 256 U.S. 208 (1921), held that proof of a written or oral contract was not necessary to establish an illegal vertical agreement. **(A) is incorrect** because the agreement might be implicit. **(B) is incorrect** because conscious parallelism applies to horizontal agreements. **(C) is the correct answer** under the rule in Sharp. **(D) is incorrect** because threats by themselves do not establish an agreement.

85. This question tests your understanding of how to show a vertical agreement. See Question 84. **(A) is the correct answer** under the rules in Monsanto and Sharp. **(B) is incorrect** because the standard is rule of reason and consumer harm is only part of the analysis of anticompetitive effects. **(C) is incorrect** because non-price agreements, like geographic restraints, are separate from price restraints. **(D) is incorrect** because there is antitrust injury through harm to competition among retailers.

86. This question tests your knowledge of the Sharp case, cited in the answer to Question 84. **(A) is incorrect** because that is not the holding of Business Electronics v Sharp. **(B) is the correct answer.** The Sharp decision is seen as making it more difficult for plaintiffs to establish a case for illegal vertical price restraints. **(C) and (D) are incorrect** because market power is not relevant.

87. This question tests your knowledge about the relationship between vertical and horizontal agreements. See the Klor's decision, cited in the answer to Question 64. The agreements at issue in Question 87 have both a horizontal and vertical dimension. Retailers agree among themselves to enter into a vertical agreement. **(A) and (C) are incorrect** because they ignore the horizontal dimension of the agreement. **(B) is the correct answer** because effectively the agreement at issue here is a horizontal one to fix price. **(D) is incorrect** because there is antitrust injury resulting to retailers under the restraint.

88. This question tests your knowledge of an exclusive distribution system. Under such a system, a manufacturer agrees to deal with only certain retailers and in exchange the retailers agree to deal with the manufacturer. This exclusive system is a combination of exclusive dealing and exclusive distributorship. An exclusive dealing is an agreement that a retailer or group of retailers will deal with only one manufacturer. An exclusive distributorship (or exclusive dealership) is an agreement that a manufacturer will deal with only one retailer. In general, exclusive distribution systems are a combination of vertical and horizontal agreements. **(A), (B), and (D) are each incorrect** because each ignores either the horizontal or vertical dimension of the agreements. **(C) is the correct answer** because it recognizes that horizontal and vertical agreements would be involved. In this case, the agreement among retailers is horizontal, and that with the manufacturers is vertical. See Question 87.

89. This question tests your knowledge of an exclusive dealership, or exclusive dealing. *See* FTC. v. Motion Picture Advertising Service, 344 U.S. 392 (1953). **(A) and (B) are both true, and, therefore, incorrect,** making **(C) the correct answer.**

90.   This question tests your knowledge of an exclusive distributorship (or exclusive dealership) and its relationship to refusals to deal. *See* Paddock v. Chicago Tribune, 103 F.3d 42 (7th Cir. 1996). Exclusive distributorships are viewed the same as vertical price and non-price interests. The limits on competition, if any, are outweighed by benefits in investing in the brand and strengthening interbrand competition. By contrast, exclusive dealing is more suspect because competing manufacturers are likely to be foreclosed from working with dealers and retailers. **(A) is the correct answer** that reflects the lower scrutiny for exclusive distributorships. **(B) is incorrect** because it ignores the benefits of exclusive dealerships. **(C) is incorrect** because there is no such immunity. **(D) is incorrect** because there is antitrust injury from potential restraints on competition.

91.   This question tests your understanding of the differences between exclusive distributorships (or exclusive dealership) and exclusive dealing. See Questions 89 and 90. **(B) is the correct answer** because it correctly identifies the difference. An exclusive dealership is a restriction on the manufacturer while an exclusive dealing is a restriction on the retailer. The other three choices, **(A), (B), and (C) misstate the definition and rules, and are therefore incorrect.** Choice (A) has it backwards in its definition of the two concepts. Choice (C) states the standard of review incorrectly. Exclusive dealerships are subject to rule of reason while exclusive dealing agreements receive greater scrutiny. Choice (D) makes the same mistake as Choice (A). Exclusive dealership restricts the manufacturer while exclusive dealing restricts the retailer.

92.   This question tests your knowledge about the differences among the various antitrust statutes in their treatment of exclusive dealing. In general, all three statutes apply but the standard is slightly different for the Clayton Act. See Question 93. Under the Federal Trade Commission Act, the ultimate question is whether the agreement is an unfair or deceptive business practice, a conclusion that requires a violation of the Sherman or Clayton Act. *See* CDC Technologies v. Idexx Labs, 186 F.3d 74 (2d Cir. 1999); Tampa Electric v. Nashville Coal Co., 365 U.S. 320 (1961). A, B, and C are each true. So **(D) is the correct answer**.

93.   The question tests your understanding of the standard under Section 3 of the Clayton Act. The answer choices highlight the critical distinctions under that section. See FTC v. Brown Shoe, 384 U.S. 316 (1966) for a comparison of the provisions. **(A) is incorrect** because the correct standard is substantially lessens competition. **(B) is incorrect** because the Clayton Act covers products, but not services. **(C) is the correct answer** because it covers the key elements. The Clayton Act covers a sale, a product, and imposes the standard of substantially lessening competition. This standard requires some consideration of the market effects of the agreement. See Tampa Electric, cited in the answer to Question 92, for an example of this market analysis. **(D) is incorrect** because the Clayton Act covers sales but not purchases.

94.   This question tests your knowledge on the differences between the Clayton Act and the Sherman Act. See Question 93. **(A) is incorrect** because requirements contracts are also covered under the Clayton Act. **(B) is the correct answer** because the Clayton Act has the standard of substantially lessening competition as opposed to comparing procompetitive and anticompetitive effects under the rule of reason. See Question 85 and the Tampa Electric case cited in the answer to Question 92. **(C) is incorrect** because treatment is not per se under the Clayton Act. **(D) is incorrect** because antitrust injury is required for both claims.

95. This question tests your knowledge of tying arrangements. *See* Jefferson Parish Hospital v. Hyde, 466 U.S. 2 (1984). **(A) is the correct answer** because it states the correct definition. **(B) is incorrect** because rule of reason may apply in some situations. **(C) is incorrect** because the per se rule would apply if there is market power in the tying product. **(D) is incorrect** because the trigger for the per se rule is market power in the tying product.

96. This question tests you knowledge of tying arrangements. See Jefferson Parish, cited in the answer to Question 95. The trigger for per se treatment is market power in the tying product, the product that the purchaser wants to buy as opposed to the one that he is required to buy because of the tie. **(A) is the correct answer** as stated in Jefferson Parish. **(B), (C) and (D) each misstate the rule, and are therefore incorrect.** Choice (B) misstates the application of rule of reason and confusingly raises market power in the tied product, which is irrelevant. Choice (C) ignores the other elements of a tying claim beyond existence of market power. Choice (D) states the exact opposite rule.

97. This question tests your understanding of how an antitrust defendant would challenge a tying claim. See Jefferson Parish cited in the answer to Question 95. **(C) is the correct answer** because a tying claim requires the showing of two distinct product or services. This issue was central to Jefferson Parish (were anesthesiological services separate from surgical services) and in Microsoft, discussed in Question 98, (were Internet Explorer and Windows one product or two). None of the others constitute a defense. **Choice (A) is irrelevant** because consent by the purchaser is not a defense to an anticompetitive contract. **Choice (B) makes no sense** for the same reason as Choice (A). If the tie was anticompetitive, consent is no a defense. **Choice (D) is incorrect** because market power in the tying product is relevant for the standard, per se or rule of reason, and to a defense for the underlying claim.

98. This question tests your knowledge of tying arrangements in a technology context. *See* United States v. Microsoft, 253 F.3d 34 (D.C. Cir. 2001). **(A) is incorrect** because Microsoft was found to have market power. **(B) is incorrect** because the court found them to be two products. **(C) is incorrect** because the court did find illegal licensing practices such as the requirement of a per processor licensing fee. **(D) is the correct answer.** The court ruled that because software is such a rapidly changing area, courts should be cautious in imposing per se rules with respect to technological ties.

99. As stated in the answer to Question 72, a horizontal agreement is one between competitors at the same level of a distribution chain while a vertical agreement is one between those at different levels of a distribution chain. The basic principle underlying antitrust scrutiny of both types of agreements is that competitors are supposed to compete with each other and not engage in collaborative conduct. As a practical matter, complete non-collaboration may be difficult if not impossible. Firms cannot always exist at arm's length. Nonetheless, the view is that antitrust law should be brought to bear in cases where firms do collaborate with each other because of the concern that competition might be compromised. Since the two types of agreement differ in terms of the parties involved and their place in the distribution chain, antitrust law has different rules for the two types of agreements with vertical agreements generally subject to the rule of reason and horizontal agreements subject in some situations to a per se rule.

100. This statement is accurate although one can find exceptions. In general, vertical agreements allow firms to work out issues of distribution such as pricing, territories, and provision of

service. Such issues are important for consumers and can yield benefits to the market. Horizontal agreements can also yield benefits, but the concern is that collaboration among horizontal competitors can lead to acts like price fixing or division of territories which would in general hurt consumers. Therefore, horizontal agreements might be more harmful than vertical ones. However, vertical agreements can be a cover for horizontal agreements. Suppose three retailers band together to make a certain manufacture refuse to supply products to a fourth retailer except on certain terms. The agreement between the manufacture and the fourth retailer might look like a vertical agreement, but it is a disguised horizontal agreement. Therefore, vertical agreements can be harmful and are not immunized from antitrust laws. They are subject to the rule of reason.

101. This question tests your knowledge of the difference between Sections One and Two of the Sherman Act. *See* Standard Oil v. United States, 221 U.S. 1 (1911). **(A), (B), and (D) are each accurate, making them incorrect. (C) is the correct answer** because the exact opposite is true. Section One requires agreement among two or more entities while Section Two requires unilateral conduct.

102. This question tests your knowledge of the elements to establish a violation of Section Two of the Sherman Act. *See* United States v. Alcoa, 148 F.2d 416 (2d Cir. 1945). **(A) is incorrect** because intent is required for attempted monopolization, but not for monopolization in general. See the materials in Chapter Eight. **(B) and (C) are incorrect** because monopolistic conduct is required. **(D) is the correct answer** because market power is an element of Section Two. A defendant is liable for monopolization only if the entity has market power (and has engaged in monopolistic conduct).

103. This question tests your knowledge of market definition and reviews concepts tested in Chapter Two. **(A) is incorrect** because market share presumes market definition. **(B) is the correct answer** because it describes elements that help to understand what the relevant market is. See the Alcoa decision cited in the answers to Question 90. **(C) is incorrect** because each factor assumes market definition. **(D) is incorrect** because number of firms and concentration assume market definition.

104. This question tests your knowledge of market definition based on cross price elasticity of demand. Chapter Two presented several review questions about elasticity. Cross price elasticity of demand measures the percentage change in quantity demanded for one product if the price of another product rises. If the price of another product rises and the quantity demanded rises, that means one product is a substitute for the other, meaning that consumers switch to the product when the price changes. For example, if the price of beef rises, the demand for chicken might rise because chicken and beef are substitutes. If two products are substitutes, they are considered to be in the same market. **(A) is incorrect** because the relationship is one of substitutes if the cross price elasticity is positive. **(B) is incorrect** because while substitutes might be in the same market, one should be careful in relying on cross price elasticity alone. **(C) is the correct answer** because other factors should be considered. **(D) is incorrect** because the relationship has some relevance to market definition but the Cellophane Fallacy has to be kept in mind for the analysis. The Cellophane fallacy is a reference to United States v. du Pont, 351 U.S. 377 (1956) in which the Court ruled that the defendant had a low market share because cellophane had a highly positive cross price elasticity with other flexible wrapping materials, implying they were substitutes and in the same market. Commentators criticized the Court's reasoning because a high cross price elasticity would be consistent with monopoly pricing in the cellophane market. While cross price elasticity is some indication, one needs to be careful in overemphasizing a high cross price elasticity as an indication of a broad market.

105. This question tests your understanding of the relationship between Section One and Section Two claims under the Sherman Act. **(D) is the correct answer** because it identifies market power as the missing element in the quoted stated. The other choices misstate the law. **(A) is wrong** because the statement is not accurate for at least the one reason already given. **(B) is wrong** because intent is not an element for either claim. **(C) is a confusing statement**. Even if the firm acting unilaterally were part of a cartel, there would be a potential basis for two separate claims under Section One for cartel and under Section Two for the unilateral conduct.

106. This question tests your knowledge of what constitutes monopolistic conduct, a requirement for a Section Two claim. There are three types of monopolistic conduct: predatory behavior, exclusionary behavior, leveraging. Predatory behavior is an act by a dominant firm to drive out existing competitors. *See* Matsushita v. Zenith, 475 U.S. 574 (1986) (predatory pricing). Exclusionary behavior is an act that tries to prevent new firms from entering into a market. *See* Verizon v. Trinko, 540 U.S. 398 (2004) (foreclosing entry into telecommunications). Leveraging is an act that extends market power over one product or service into another. Tying would be one example. See Chapter Five. *See also* Berkey Photo v. Eastman Kodak, 603 F.2d 263 (2d Cir. 1979) (allegedly designing cameras in order to extend market power in film to camera market). **(A) is the correct answer** because it describes predatory behavior. **(B) is incorrect** because acquiring patents alone is not a violation. **(C) is incorrect** because a stable market share is not a violation. **(D) is incorrect** because exclusive licensing is not a violation.

107. This question tests your knowledge of the Alcoa discussion, cited in the answer to Question 102. **(A) is incorrect** because Judge Hand did not include foreign supply. **(B) is the correct answer** because it states correctly how Judge Hand defined the market to exclude second hand, or used, aluminum. **(C) is incorrect** because Judge Hand found the acquisition of market power to be illegal. **(D) is incorrect** because Judge Hand found the opposite for the attempted monopolization claim.

108. This question tests your knowledge of the Alcoa decision where the concept of excess capacity arose. Excess capacity refers to unused or idle plant and equipment that would allow a firm to increase production. The idea is that the firm creates excess capacity in order to reduce output (and thereby raise price in the market). In addition, a firm might retain excess capacity in order to increase output once competitors are driven out. **(A) is incorrect** because there is no per se violation under Section Two. **(B) is incorrect** because unilateral conduct is not a Section One violation. **(C) is the correct answer** based on the Alcoa decision in which the court found that the antitrust defendant was retaining excess capacity in order to meet market demand once competitors exited. **(D) is incorrect** because skill and foresight are irrelevant for the analysis.

109. This question tests your knowledge about market power. **(A) is the correct statement** because market power has to be in the same market where there is antitrust injury. *See* Aquatherm v. Florida Power & Light, 145 F.3d 1258 (11th Cir. 1998); Intergraph v. Intel, 195 F.3d 1346 (Fed. Cir. 1999). **(B) is incorrect** because past market power may be the basis for a past violation. **(C) is incorrect** because market power is an element however obtained. **(D) is incorrect** because current market power may be the basis for a current violation.

110. This question tests your understanding of the economics and policy behind Section Two

claims. It reviews concepts from Chapter Two. **(A) is incorrect** because the problem is too few firms, not too many. **(B) is the correct answer**. Because a firm with market power faces little or no competition, it can raise price based on market demand and reduce output. Deadweight loss refers to the sales that would occur if there was perfect competition but are not realized by a firm with market power that maximizes profits by charging a higher than competitive price to fewer consumers. **(C) is incorrect** because large firms sometimes can promote innovation. **(D) is incorrect** because the problem is too high a price, not too low a price.

111. This question tests your knowledge of monopsony. *See* United States v. Griffith, 334 U.S. 100 (1948) (single movie theaters in small towns as monopsonist in buying movies for exhibition); Weyerhaueser v. Ross-Simmons, 549 U.S. 312 (2007) (dominant purchaser of lumber). **(B) is the correct answer** because it states the correct definition (one buyer) and the implications for the market (the one buyer has market power to purchase at too low a price). The other choices misstate the definition or the law. **(A) is incorrect** because it describes what is known as a bilateral monopoly. A monopsony is a market that is the mirror of a monopoly: one buyer and many sellers. **(C) is incorrect** as the cases cited in this paragraph show. **(D) is incorrect** because the elements of Section Two apply; there must a finding of market power and illegal conduct.

112. This question tests your understanding of an oligopoly, a market with a few dominant firms. **(A) is incorrect** because there is no such immunity. **(B) is incorrect** because an oligopoly is a different market structure from a monopoly. **(C) is the correct answer** because agreement among these firms would be the basis for a Section One claim. **(D) is incorrect** because the scenario is not the only one creating potential liability.

113. This question tests your understanding of an oligopoly. *See* duPont v. FTC, 729 F.2d 128 (1984). **(A) is incorrect** because Section Two applies to the action of one firm, not a group of firms. **(B) is the correct answer** because oligopoly conduct is subject to all of the antitrust law, the Sherman Act, the Clayton Act, and the FTCA. **(C) is incorrect** because other provisions of the antitrust laws are applicable. **(D) is incorrect** because the market may not be efficient.

114. This question tests your knowledge of the relationship between antitrust and intellectual property laws. **(A) is incorrect** because of the rule in Illinois Tool v. Independent Ink, 547 U.S. 28 (2006) (holding that there is no presumption of market power from ownership of a patent). **(B) is the correct answer** because antitrust laws apply to owners of intellectual property. **(C) is incorrect** because ownership of a patent by itself is not a violation. **(D) is incorrect** because there is no such immunity.

115. This question tests your knowledge of remedies for a violation of Section Two. The statute spells these remedies out clearly. See the Microsoft case, cited in the answer to Question 98, for a discussion of remedies. **(A), (B), and (C) are each remedies, and, therefore, incorrect. (D) is the correct answer**.

116. A Section One claim requires two or more entities engaging in an anticompetitive agreement. A Section Two claim, by contrast, deals with unilateral conduct. A Section One claim does not require a showing of market power by the defendants while a Section Two claim does. Both claims address conduct that hurts market competition. Section One covers

collusive behavior by firms that excludes competitors, raises prices, and reduces the quality of the product. Section Two covers behavior by one firm who can exclude competitors, raise prices and reduce quality because of market power.

117.   Market power is the ability of a firm or consumer to affect the price in the marketplace. In a perfectly competitive market, no firm or consumer has the ability to affect price. Instead, the market price is determined by the competitive interactions of firms and consumers. However, if a firm or consumer can engage in conduct that affects market price, then the form or consumer is said to have market power. The presence of such a firm or consumer distorts a perfectly competitive market, requiring enforcement of the antitrust laws through a Section Two claim.

118.   This question tests your understanding of what conduct is actionable under Section Two. See the answer to Question 106 for more details. **(A) is incorrect** because restraint of trade is relevant under Section One. **(B) is incorrect** because a bad act is required. **(C) is the correct answer**. See answer to Question 106 as review. **(D) is incorrect** because economic inefficiency is not a legal requirement.

119.   This question tests your understanding of what constitutes exclusionary conduct that entails a violation of Section Two of the Sherman Act. See the answer to Question 106 for further review. **(A) is the correct answer** because it provides an example of what constitutes market exclusion. *See* United States v. Terminal Railway, 224 U.S. 383 (1912). **(B) is incorrect** because it describes leveraging. **(C) is incorrect** because it describes price fixing. **(D) is incorrect** because it describes leveraging.

120.   This question tests your knowledge about leveraging, a basis for showing monopolistic conduct. See the answer to Question 106 for further details. **(A) is incorrect** because it describes exclusionary conduct. **(B) is the correct answer** because it correctly states that leveraging involves using a monopoly position to expand into other markets. **(C) is incorrect** because it describes price fixing which is actionable under Section One. **(D) is incorrect** because it describes tying, one example of leveraging but not the only one.

121.   This question tests your understanding of the Alcoa decision, discussed in the answers to Questions 102, 103, 107 and 108. **(A) is incorrect** because there was no such finding. **(B) is the correct answer** because the judge did find that Alcoa created excess capacity in order to meet the market after competitors were forced out. **(C) is incorrect** because there was no such leveraging. **(D) is incorrect** because there was no Section One claim of price fixing.

122.   This question tests your understanding of Section Two of the Sherman Act, especially its limitations. **(A) is the correct answer**. The Microsoft case is one basis for this criticism. Many of Microsoft's licensing practices were beneficial to developing Windows and Internet Explorer for the sake of consumers. **(B) is incorrect** because an agreement is the basis for a Section One claim, not Section Two. **(C) is incorrect** because joint ventures are analyzed under Section One. **(D) is incorrect** because vertical restraints are analyzed under Section One.

123.   The question tests your knowledge of United States v. United Shoe, 110 F. Supp. 295 (D. Mass. 1953), a district court decision affirmed without opinion by the United States Supreme Court. The case is important because it illustrates licensing practices used by a firm to maintain its dominant position through exclusionary practices. **(A) is incorrect** because there was no such thing. **(B) is the correct answer**. The court ruled that by not permitting purchases, United Shoe was limiting competition from used machines. Licensing also required customers to rely on United Shoe for service and other features which made it

more difficult more other firms to compete. **(C) is incorrect** because there was no such conduct at issue. **(D) is incorrect** because there was no such conduct at issue.

124. This question tests your knowledge of leveraging theories of monopolistic conduct, as illustrated by the Berkey Photo case, cited in the answer to Question 96. **(A) is the correct answer.** Berkey was accused of developed a camera that could only be used with its film, in which the company had market power. The court rejected the claim, however. **(B) is incorrect** because such predisclosure is what the plaintiff was seeking. **(C) is incorrect** because there was no such conduct at issue. **(D) is incorrect** because there was no such conduct at issue.

125. This question tests your understanding of technological ties and antitrust issues rising from new technologies. The Berkey case, examined in Questions 106 and 124, illustrate these points. **(A) is incorrect** because liability is not automatic. **(B) is incorrect** because the standard is relevant for attempted monopolization, which may not be the relevant claim. **(C) is incorrect** because there is no immunity from liability. **(D) is the correct answer** with the additional abusive conduct being key. The additional abusive conduct would be an exclusionary or predatory practice, such as anticompetitive licensing practices as in the Microsoft case.

126. This question tests your knowledge of exclusionary conduct, especially refusals to deal with other firms. The key case is Aspen Skiing v. Aspen Highlands, 472 U.S. 585 (1985), in which a skiing company with market power refused to further cooperate with a competitor in marketing a group ticket. The Court upheld the finding of a violation. See also Otter Tail v. United States, 410 U.S. 366 (1973), in which the Court discussed the essential facilities doctrine and its limited role in U.S. antitrust law. **(A), (C), and (D) are each accurate, and, therefore, incorrect.** (A) is generally true. (C) and (D) illustrate the rule from Aspen Skiing. **(B) is the correct answer** because there is no duty to cooperate under the antitrust laws.

127. This question tests your understanding of the essential facilities doctrine, discussed in the Otter Tail decision cited in the answer to Question 126. **(A) is incorrect** because the doctrine is not often applied and may not even exist in the U.S. **(B) is incorrect** because there is no duty to cooperate. **(C) is correct** because it reflects the analysis in Otter Tail as it interprets the Terminal Railway decision. **(D) is incorrect** because there is no exemption from the antitrust laws for intellectual property owners.

128. This question tests your understanding of refusals to deal as exclusionary conduct. The key here is that the company that used to deal with retailers now refuses to, in order to strengthen its position in the retailing sector. **(A) is incorrect** because vertical integration is actionable. **(B) is incorrect** because market power may not be extended or leveraged as described. **(C) is incorrect** because it misstates the essential facility doctrine. There is no evidence of an essential facility under these facts. **(D) is the correct answer** because the issue would be the effect of the firm's conduct on monopolizing the retailing market.

129. This question tests your knowledge of vertical integration, which arises when one firm merges or acquires another firm that is in the chain of distribution. *See* Paschall v. Kansas City Star, 727 F.2d 692 (8th Cir. 1984) (newspaper allowed to terminate independent carriers and replace them with own delivery service despite antitrust challenge). **(A) and (C) are incorrect** because there is no per se legal category. **(B) is the correct answer** because an

antitrust challenge to a vertical integration will look at this effects and consider business justifications for why integration makes the market work better. **(D) is incorrect** because the rationale stated makes no sense. Lowering barriers to entry would make it more difficult to establish market power.

130. This question tests your understanding of a price squeeze. The Alcoa decision, cited in the answer to Question 102, illustrates a price squeeze and is the basis for the scenario in this question. *See also* Bonjorno v. Kaiser Aluminum, 752 F.d 802 (3d Cir. 1984). **(C) is the correct answer** because such refusal to deal is not a defense to predatory conduct. **(A), (B), and (D) are accurate, and, therefore, incorrect.**

131. This question tests your understanding of a price squeeze and is a follow-up to Question 130. **(A) is incorrect** because the concern is the gain in market power that can result in higher prices in the future. **(B) is incorrect** because the theory underlying the illegality of a price squeeze is predatory conduct, not leveraging. **(C) is the correct answer.** For the price squeeze to be predatory, it has to reduce competition in the marketplace and the scheme has to have some probability of success. **(D) is incorrect** because higher prices are not inevitable.

132. This question tests your knowledge of the Otter Tail decision as it illustrates various theories of monopolistic conduct. See the discussion in the answer to Questions 126 and 127. A, B, and D are each incorrect because each misstates the law. **(C) is the correct answer** because Otter Tail's liability rested on vertically integrating energy supply and generation in a way that limited competition in the market.

133. This question tests your knowledge of telecommunications deregulation and of procedural developments in antitrust litigation. *See* Trinko, cited in the answer to Question 106, and Bell Atlantic v. Twombly, 127 S. Ct. 1955 (2007) (holding that theory of antitrust agreement had to be plausible in order to survive a 12(b)(6) motion). **(A) is incorrect** because antitrust claims are more difficult to bring in light of Trinko and Twombly. **(B) is the correct answer** because it explains how Trinko and Twombly together have changed the landscape. **(C) is incorrect** because there is no express language in the Act. **(D) is incorrect** because while it may state a correct principle in the abstract, it does not represent how courts have approached the deregulated telecommunications industry.

134. This question tests your understanding of the concept of raising rivals' cost, which arises when a firm tries to make it more expensive for a rival to compete in the marketplace. An example might be obtaining a patent on a needed technology or refusal to sell or provide an input to production. **(A) is incorrect** because it can explain both. **(B) is incorrect** because there is no such rule. **(C) is the correct answer** because both cases illustrate how a dominant firm can make it more expensive for a rival to compete because of differential costs. **(D) is incorrect** because the court did not adopt such a rule.

135. This question tests your understanding of the Microsoft case, cited in the answer to Question 100. **(A) is incorrect** because market power was found. **(B) is incorrect** because they were found to be two products, not one. **(C) is the correct answer** because the court ruled that a more deferential standard was appropriate for software based tying claims. **(D) is incorrect** because there is no such rule. The court held that rule of reason would apply to ties involving software.

136.   This question tests your understanding of tying arrangements and the relationship between Section One and Section Two claims. **(A) is incorrect** because Section One may also apply. **(B) is incorrect** because there is no such rule. **(C) is the correct answer.** *See Jefferson Parish*, the case cited in the answer to Question 95. **(D) is incorrect** because market power in the tied product is not relevant.

137.   This question tests your understanding of tying arrangements. **(A), (C), and (D) are each examples, making them incorrect.** Choice (A) illustrates the claim in Illinois Tool, the case cited in the answer to Question 104. Choice (C) illustrates the claim in Eastman Kodak v. Image Technical Services, 504 U.S. 451 (1992). Choice (D) illustrates the claim in Fortner Enterprises v. United States, 394 U.S. 495 (1969). **(B) is the correct answer** because these individual products constitute one product with respect to the franchise. *See Krehl*, cited in answer to Question 78.

138.   This question tests your understanding of tying arrangements. Many previous questions illustrate these points. See answers to Questions 95, 106, and 114. **(A) is incorrect** because market power is required for the per se rule. **(B) is incorrect** because there are two products here. **(C) is incorrect** because there is no per se rule of market power arising from patent ownership. **(D) is the correct answer** because it states the general rule for the analysis of tying arrangements, which would be applicable here.

139.   This question tests your knowledge of tying arrangements, particularly the specific practice of block booking which was at issue in United States v. Loew's, 371 U.S. 38 (1962). **(A) is the correct answer** because it states the correct categorization of the practice. **(B) is incorrect** because booking is practice and not a facility. **(C) is incorrect** because the issue was of leveraging and not predation. **(D) is incorrect** because there is no per se legal category.

140.   This question tests your understanding of monopsony. See discussion in answer to Question 111. **(A) is incorrect** because there is no exemption. **(B) is incorrect** because there is no lower standard. **(C) is the correct answer** because it states the policy reasons for why a monopsony can be illegal in violation of Section Two of the Sherman Act. **(D) is incorrect** because monopsonies can be harmful.

141.   This question tests your understanding of Section Two of the Sherman Act and what constitutes monopolistic conduct. **(A) is incorrect** because pricing by itself does not constitute monopolistic conduct. **(B) is the correct answer** because a price increase by itself is not monopolistic conduct. **(C) is incorrect** because the Sherman Act does not make pricing alone actionable. **(D) is incorrect** because it understates the point that pricing along is not actionable.

142.   This question tests your understanding of market power, as applied to a monopsonist. **(A) is the correct answer**. See Griffith, discussed in answer to Question 111. **(B) is incorrect** because supply is the relevant side of the market when there is only one buyer. **(C) is incorrect** because this mark-up is relevant for a monopolist, not a monopsonist. **(D) is incorrect** because it vaguely refers to the conditions for predatory pricing.

143.   Exclusionary conduct is conduct that keeps competitors from entering a market. An example would be setting a market standard that a new firm cannot meet. Predatory conduct is conduct that is designed to preserve market power and raise price. An example would be

lowering the market price to drive out competitors and preserve or establish market power. Leveraging entails using market power in one market to establish market power in another. An example would be a tying arrangement.

144. Under antitrust law, it is not illegal to be a monopolist. However, it is illegal to use market power in engage in conduct that is anticompetitive and harmful to the market. The reason is that antitrust law is not designed to penalize market success, and a monopoly may very well be the result of developing a superior product, business acumen, or just luck. However, if a market is competitive, any firm should be able to obtain market success. Therefore, antitrust law penalizes monopolistic conduct that prevents competition which can allow the entry of new firms.

TOPIC 8:	ANSWERS
ATTEMPTED MONOPOLIZATION	

145. This question tests your basic understanding of the requirements for a claim of attempted monopolization. See Spectrum Sports, Inc. v. McQuillan, 506 U.S. 447 (1993), for a discussion of the elements and background to the claim. **(D) is the correct answer** because it accurately states the rule from Spectrum Sports. The other choices misstate the rule. **Choice (A) is incorrect** because it fails to mention that specific intent is an element of the offense. **Choice (B) is incorrect** because the conduct need not show a specific intent. Instead, specific intent is separate from the showing of conduct and can be based on subjective elements, as the questions below show. **Choice (C) is incorrect** because the standard is one of specific intent, not gross recklessness.

146. This question tests your understanding of the specific intent prong of an attempted monopolization claim. Specific intent means that there was knowledge or purpose in monopolizing a market. Specific intent can be shown by a pattern of conduct and by subjective intention. See William Inglis v. ITT Continental Bakery, 668 F.2d 1014 (9th Cir. 1981); United States v. Empire Gas Co., 537 F.2d 296 (8th Cir. 1976). **(A), (C), and (D) are each accurate, and, therefore, incorrect.** Pattern of conduct can be a basis to establish intent. But remember that conduct is a separate element from intent as well. **(B) is the correct answer** because subjective hopes are not sufficient to show intent.

147. This question tests your understanding of the dangerous probability of success element of an attempted monopolization claim. Although language from Swift v. United States, 196 U.S. 375 (1905), that intent and dangerous probability are overlapped elements, the analysis of market effects and the likelihood of success in Lorrain Journal v. United States, 342 U.S. 143 (1951), shows that intent and dangerous probability are distinct elements. Therefore, **(D) is the correct answer**. The two elements need to be shown separately. **The other three choices, (A), (B), and (C), are incorrect** because they confuse the two elements.

148. This question tests your understanding of market power in a claim for attempted monopolization. *See Lorrain Journal*, cited in the answer to Question 147. **(A) is incorrect** because market power is relevant. **(B) is the correct answer** because it states the correct proposition that market definition is a prerequisite to determining dangerous probability of success. **(C) is incorrect** because the elements are separate. **(D) is incorrect** because market definition is not relevant to the intent of the defendant.

149. This question tests your understanding of market share analysis in a claim for attempted monopolization. It is a variation of Question 148. **(A) is the correct answer** because it makes the point that a high market share means that defendant's conduct is more likely to be successful in monopolizing a market. **(B) is incorrect** because specific intent is a separate element. **(C) is incorrect** because adverse effects on consumers are not relevant to the elements of the claim. **(D) is incorrect** because market power is not a separate element of the claim.

150.   This question tests your understanding of leveraging as a theory of monopolistic conduct for an attempted monopolization claim. See the answer to Question 106. *See also Berkey Photo*, discussed in answer to Question 106, and Alaska Airlines v. United Airlines, 948 F.2d 546 (9th Cir. 1991) (attempted monopolization through computerized reservation system). **(A) is incorrect** because predatory and leveraging theories can be separate. **(B) is the correct answer** because it states the correct elements. **(C) is incorrect** because there is no duty to cooperate. **(D) is incorrect** because the answer describes exclusionary conduct.

151.   This question tests your understanding of predatory pricing as a basis for a claim of attempted monopolization. A predatory pricing is the allegation that the defendant lowered its prices in order to drive out competition with the intent to increase prices when a monopoly was established. The theory is controversial because of its economic plausibility. For such a scheme to work, a firm would have to set prices sometimes way below costs, resulting in a loss of profit. The price drop would then have to drive out competitors. Finally, the firm would have to be able to raise prices sufficiently to recoup the earlier losses. *See Matsushita*, cited in answer to Question 106. **(A) is incorrect** because predation occurs in the same market, not a related one. Predation is different from leveraging that requires two separate markets. **(B) is incorrect** because the concern is not that prices are low for a long period of time, but that prices are increased. **(C) is the correct answer** because under Matsushita, the plaintiff would have to show that the defendant would be able to recoup losses from the predatory behavior. **(D) is incorrect** because the concern is that firms sometimes may not be able to enter and that dominant firm can raise prices.

152.   This question tests your understanding of the economics of predatory pricing. The economics forms the basis for the legal treatment of predatory pricing. The economic elements are pricing below marginal cost to deter entry followed by monopoly pricing, namely pricing as a mark-up of marginal cost after firms have been driven out. **(A) is the correct answer** because it states these elements. **(B) is incorrect** because of demand does not respond to price, the strategy of predation through price is less likely to work. **(C) is incorrect** because pricing needs to be below the profit maximizing level in the short run and above it in the long run. **(D) is incorrect** because excess capacity will aid a firm in predation.

153.   This question tests your understanding of the mechanics of a predatory pricing scheme. **(B) is the correct answer** because if there is unused plants and equipment, the predating firm can readily increase output to reduce price and drive out competition. The other answers are examples of what would make predation less likely to be successful. Under Choice (A), very little excess capacity will make it more difficult for a firm to lower prices and steal customers from competitors. Under Choice (C), if entry of new firms is easy, then new firms will enter when the predatory firm raises price and therefore make his scheme more difficult to implement. Under Choice (D), if consumers are not sensitive to price, which these facts suggest, then the predating firm will less likely steal away customers from competitors by lowering price.

154.   This question tests your understanding of how a plaintiff would prove predatory pricing. In general marginal cost is impossible to measure. Consequently, a plaintiff has to use a proxy like average cost to identify pricing behavior consistent with a predatory pricing theory. **(B) is correct** because it states the test often used. This measure is associated with Areeda and Turner and is the focus of Question 155. **(A) is incorrect** because the relevant comparison is with average or marginal cost, that is cost expressed per unit of quantity. **(C) is incorrect**

because price equal to marginal cost is the profit maximizing level and the theory is that price is below the marginal cost. **(D) is incorrect** because the theory is that the firm is operating at a loss and so price must be below average variable cost.

155. This question tests your understanding of how a plaintiff would prove predatory pricing. The central problem with the use of average total cost, and with predatory pricing as a theory of attempted monopolization, is that lowering prices helps consumers. Evidence of low prices is consistent with both vigorous competition and with predatory behavior. **(A) is incorrect** because the measure does not look to marginal cost. **(B) is the correct answer** indicating the ambiguity of the evidence. **(C) is incorrect** because the test does not address recoupment directly. **(D) is incorrect** because sometimes efficient behavior is deterred under the test.

156. This question tests your understanding of a predatory buying case, which is the mirror image of a predatory pricing claim in a monopsony market. See Weyerhaeuser, the case cited in the answer to Question 111. **(A) is incorrect** since the standards are the same. **(B) is incorrect** because the claim is exactly the opposite as stated in C. **(C) is the correct answer**. A buyer overbids to obtain control over an input and then dries out competitors to obtain a monopsony in the market. **(D) is incorrect** because the standards are the same.

157. This question tests your understanding of a practice called bundling, which arises in attempted monopolization cases. *See* LaPage's v. 3M Corp., 224 F.3d 141 (3d Cir. 2002); Cascade Health Solutions v. PeaceHealth, 502 F.3d 895 (9th Cir. 2007). **(A) is incorrect** because the practice can be actionable. **(B) is incorrect** because as a tying arrangement, the per se rule may apply. **(C) is the correct answer** because the legal theory is one of predation. The problem is the difficulty of measuring the relevant cost for the bundled set of products. **(D) is incorrect** because as a tying arrangement, the rule of reason may apply.

158. This question tests your understanding of conspiracy to monopolize. The main issue is whether a market analysis is required for a claim of conspiracy as for an attempt claim under Spectrum Sports. *See* Nynex v. Discon, Inc., 525 U.S. 128 (1998) for a discussion of conspiracy and market analysis. **(A), (B), and (D) each misstate the law, making them incorrect. (C) is the correct answer** which states the formal legal requirements. Choice (A) confuses attempt claims with conspiracy claims. Choice (B) states the elements for an attempt claim. Choice (D) is incorrect because a conspiracy is a distinct claim from a restraint of trade under Section One.

159. The question tests your understanding of what a plaintiff must show to establish a predatory pricing claim under Matsushita, cited in the answer to Question 106. **(A) is incorrect** because the plaintiff would have to show the possibility of recoupment. **(B) is incorrect** because specific intent could be inferred from the below average cost pricing. **(C) is the correct answer**. The plaintiff would have to show that there is a probability of success in the scheme by the defendant being able to raise prices and recoup losses. **(D) is incorrect** because there is no such burden shifting rule.

160. Market power is not required for a successful claim of attempted monopolization. The plaintiff bringing a claim of attempted monopolization has to show that there is a dangerous probability of success that a firm will result in monopolization. The presence of market power may affect this probability. If a firm has market power, then conduct may more likely

result in monopolization by the firm. However, the lack of market power does not completely negate an attempted monopolization claim. A firm might be able to gain market power by engaging in conduct that drives out competitors.

161. A predatory pricing claim entails showing that a firm has priced below average variable cost in order to drive out competitors who cannot compete and thereby obtain a monopoly position that allows the firm to raise prices. Under the Matsushita decision, there is doubt that such a claim is economically plausible. The claim assumes that the firm will suffer negative profits for an extended period of time and can recoup these lost profits through higher prices in the future. Recoupment may not be possible. Furthermore, when the firm raises prices, it is very likely that new firms will enter in response unless barriers to entry are high. Therefore, conditions must be very particular for a predatory pricing claim to be economically plausible.

162. This question tests your understanding of the different types of mergers, horizontal, conglomerate, and vertical. *See* Brown Shoe v. United States, 370 U.S. 294 (1962); FTC v. Proctor & Gamble, Co., 386 U.S. 568 (1965); United States v. Continental Can Co., 378 U.S. 441 (1964). **(B) is the correct answer** because it states accurately the economic and policy analysis of mergers as foreclosing competitions. Horizontal mergers foreclose competition among direct competitors while vertical mergers foreclose competition in distribution. The other choices, **(A), (C), and (D), are misstatements, and, therefore, incorrect.** Choice (A) is misleading because both types of mergers can produce efficiencies and costs savings, but the choice ignores market foreclosure that can arise from either type of merger. Choice (C) also emphasizes the efficiencies and understates market foreclosure. Choice (D) makes a similar mistake by assuming that the efficiencies outweigh the loss in competition. The balance of the benefits and costs of mergers depends on the market situation and industry.

163. This question tests your understanding of how courts viewed mergers under the antitrust laws. *See* Northern Securities, Inc. v. United States, 193 U.S. 197 (1904) (announcing a strict standard against mergers); Standard Oil v. United States, 221 U.S. 1 (1911) (striking down a merger under the rule of reason). **(A) is the correct answer** because it describes accurately the movement from Northern Securities to Standard Oil. **(B) is incorrect** because initially the courts adopted a strict approach, ignoring market realities. **(C) is incorrect** because there was no such set of rules. **(D) is incorrect** because mergers and acquisitions were viewed equivalently.

164. This question tests your understanding of the Clayton Act, particularly Section Seven which governs mergers. The Clayton Act was enacted in 1914 in response to the view that courts were being more lenient in antitrust enforcement. **(A) is incorrect** because there was no difference in approaches. **(B) is the correct answer** because the original act did make this distinction. **(C) is incorrect** because the requirement was one of foreclosing competition. **(D) is incorrect** because the standard at the time was a strict one ignoring economic realities.

165. This question tests your understanding of the Clayton Act and amendments made to strengthen antitrust review of mergers. **(C) is the correct answer** because the amendments made clear the standard for all mergers was one of substantially lessening competition. **(A), (B), and (D) are untrue.** Choice (A) is inaccurate because the standard was not lowered. Choice (B) is wrong because the FTC already had jurisdiction over mergers before the amendments. Choice (D) is wrong because the amendments did not impose this requirement. They arose under case law and under the 1982, 1984, and 1992 merger guidelines.

166. This question tests your knowledge of the language of the Clayton Act. **(A), (C), and (D) are each incorrect** because private parties can bring suits. **(B) is the correct answer** because

divestiture remedy is available to private plaintiffs in some situations.

167.   This question tests your understanding of the Hart-Scott-Rodino amendments to the Clayton Act. **(A) is incorrect** because the Act did not exist in 1890. **(B) is the correct answer** because the important change to the law made by the amendments were the reporting and disclosure requirements. **(C) is incorrect** because the standard is one of anticompetitive effects. **(D) is incorrect** because the Department had such authority before the Act.

168.   This question tests your understanding of the Hart-Scott-Rodino amendments to the Clayton Act. The language of the act makes clear the authority of the Department of Justice and state attorneys general as well as the disclosure requirements. **(A), (B), and (C) are each incorrect. (D) is the correct answer.**

169.   This question tests your knowledge of the failing firm defense, a judicially created defense to an antitrust claim brought against a merger. The defense has its origins in Citizen Publishing v. United States, 394 U.S. 131 (1969). The defense is established if the acquired firm's resources were so depleted that it would have left the industry and attempts to sell the firm to a noncompetitor or a less dominant competitor failed. **(A) is incorrect** because the firm need not be bankrupt. **(B) is incorrect** because the defense does not depend on the HHI. **(C) is the correct answer** because it states the elements of the defense under Citizen Publishing. **(D) is incorrect** because it misstates the rule.

170.   This question tests your knowledge of how merger analysis applies to a joint venture created by two competitors. The analysis is one of the effects of the joint venture on potential entry to the market. *See* United States v. Penn Olin, 378 U.S. 158 (1964). **(A) is incorrect** because there is no per se lawful category. **(B) is the correct answer** because it states the correct test under Penn Olin for analysis of potential entry. **(C) is incorrect** because efficiencies alone do not determine legality. **(D) is incorrect** because the rule is more specific, as stated in answer B.

171.   This question tests your understanding of the HHI, an economic concept adopted by the DoJ and the FTC in their merger guidelines. **(D) is the correct answer. (A), (B), and (C) are incorrect definitions.**

172.   This question tests your understanding of the how the HHI is used under the merger guidelines. **(B) is the correct answer** since an HHI of about 1500 is considered concentrated. **(A), (C), and (D) do not reflect this rule, and are therefore incorrect.**

173.   This question tests your knowledge of how the HHI is used under the merger guidelines. Increases in HHI in concentrated industries are more likely to be challenged. **(B) is correct** because it reflects this rule, while the others do not. **(C) is incorrect** because strict scrutiny is not accurate. Defenses may still save the merger.

174.   This question tests your understanding of the merger guidelines. **(A) is incorrect** because the HHI may be relevant, but is not the only or best factor. **(B) is the correct answer** because the guidelines require the agencies to undertake a market analysis to gauge the effect on competition. **(C) is incorrect** because there is no such abrogation. **(D) is incorrect** because potential competition is relevant.

175. This question tests your knowledge of the merger guidelines and the treatment of barriers to entry. **(A) is incorrect** because returns to scale is relevant to barriers to entry. **(B) is incorrect** because the agency will consider technological barriers. **(C) is the correct answer** because a test endorsed by the guidelines is to gauge how responsive the market would be to price increase. **(D) is incorrect** because while the HHI is relevant, it does not help identify barriers to entry.

176. This question tests your knowledge of the merger guidelines and the treatment of efficiencies. **(A) is incorrect** because it is an overstatement. Efficiencies are a factor to consider and do not immunize mergers from review. **(B) is the correct answer** because it accurately states how efficiencies are a factor in the analysis. **(C) is incorrect** because efficiencies are not presumed. **(D) is incorrect** because the merger is considered as whole not simply in terms of relative benefits and costs.

177. Mergers and acquisitions can lead to increased concentration in a market. Through a merger, two firms become one firm, potentially reducing market competition. Through an acquisition, one firm can purchase another company and its critical assets, also potentially affecting market competition. Antitrust scrutiny is needed to ensure that a specific merger or acquisition does not unduly forestall competition. Notice and reporting requirements by the companies can provide information about market effects. The Department of Justice or Federal Trade Commission can use this information to determine whether antitrust action is required to challenge the market as anticompetitive. If the merger or acquisition would be anticompetitive, the government can enjoin the transaction. Alternatively, the government can restructure the transaction to prevent or mitigate the anticompetitive harms.

178. Mergers and acquisitions are desirable because it allows companies to pool financial, physical, and intellectual assets in order to develop products and better serve consumers. Some companies may have synergies arising from the know-how, experiences, and acumen of the individuals within the companies, such as research scientists. These synergies can be tapped through a combination of the two companies through a merger or acquisition. On the other hand, mergers and acquisitions can lead to market concentration and monopolization. The costs of mergers and acquisitions are the ones associated with market concentration and monopolization: higher prices for consumers, poorer service, and potentially less innovation as the combined companies face less competitive pressures.

179. This question tests your understanding of the economics of price discrimination. An implicit assumption in the economic theory of markets is that the same product or service sells for the same price across the different transactions between buyers and sellers. This implicit assumption is not true in practice. Airline seats for the same class of service and route can be priced very differently depending on when someone buys the ticket and on when one returns. Movie tickets vary depending on the time of day. Cell phone rates can vary depending upon the plan or time of the call. These differences in price reflect the practice of price discrimination. There are different types of price discrimination. First degree price discrimination entails each consumer paying what he or she is willing to pay. Second degree price discrimination entails pricing based on the quantity of goods purchased, with higher bulk going at a lower per unit price. Third degree price discrimination entails dividing customers into groups, such as business travelers and tourists, or those above the age of 65 and those below, and charging different prices to the two groups. Price discrimination has both benefits and costs. The benefit is it keeps some consumers from being priced out of the marketplace because they can only afford a price below the going rate. On the cost side is the use of pre-discrimination to preserve or create a monopoly position. These questions aid in your understanding of the background economics to the law.

(A) is incorrect because goods of different quality may sell for different prices. **(B) is incorrect** because goods may sell for different prices at different points in time. **(C) is incorrect** because if the same discount is given to all consumers, there is no discrimination. **(D) is the correct answer** because it captures the important elements of the concept.

180. This question tests your understanding of the economics of price discrimination. See the answer to Question 179 for further details. **(D) is the correct answer.** It is inaccurate because it makes a general statement that overlooks the fact the sometimes price discrimination may harm consumers. **(A), (B), and (C) are incorrect statements.** Choice (A) correctly defines first degree price discrimination and recognizes that by charging each consumer what he or she is willing to pay, the firm extracts all the consumer surplus, i.e., no consumer gets a deal by paying less than the maximum of what he or she would be willing to pay. Choice (B) recognizes the correct definition of second degree price discrimination and the benefit of providing more output to the market than what a non-price discriminating firm would do. Choice (C) recognizes that price discrimination may make consumers better or worse off. By segmenting the market into groups, a price-discriminating firm may harm certain groups by charging more than what they would pay in a non-price-discrimination market.

181. This question tests your understanding of the economics of price discrimination. **(D) is the correct answer** because it applies the definition of third degree price discrimination. The company has segments the market into two groups. If the two groups receive the same product but at different prices, third degree price discrimination is present. **(A) is incorrect**

because if the versions have different features, then there is no price discrimination. **(B) is incorrect** because first degree requires charging each individual consumer a separate price. **(C) is incorrect** because second degree price discrimination requires differential pricing based on differences in quantity sold.

182.   This question tests your knowledge of the policy behind the Robinson-Patman, the main statutory provisions in the Clayton Act that govern price discrimination. For a good overview, see Brooke Group v. Brown & Williamson, 509 U.S. 209 (1993). **(C) is the correct answer** because the original goal was to protect small retail firms from large chains (such as A&P Groceries) which would strike favorable deals with suppliers through reduced prices and thereby shut out the smaller stores. The other choices misstate the Act's goal in protecting small retailers from large national chains. **Choice (A) is incorrect** because it states the goal was to help large chains. **Choice (B) is incorrect** because it states that goal was to prevent collusion among small stores.

   Choice (D) is incorrect because it states that the final customers were the group being aided. None of these are true as a matter of policy. Even though customers can sue, their injury is viewed as secondary line and is not the direct basis for a Robinson-Patman claim.

183.   This question tests your understanding of injury under the Robinson-Patman Act. **(A) is incorrect** because primary line is injury to competitors. *See* Utah Pie v. Continental Baking, 386 U.S. 685 (1967). **(B) is incorrect** because secondary line is injury to direct customers. *See* FTC v. Morton Salt, 334 U.S. 37 (1948). **(C) is the correct answer** because it states the correct definition of tertiary line injury. *See* Perkins v. Standard Oil, 395 U.S. 642 (1969). **(D) is incorrect** because the injury is not that broad. Choice (D) refers to claims of collusion and monopolization under the Clayton Act.

184.   This question tests your understanding of the policy behind the Robinson-Patman Act criticisms. *See* Brooke Group, cited in answer to Question 182, for a discussion. **(A) is incorrect** because it confuses price discrimination with discrimination based on race or gender. The civil rights laws do not deal with price discrimination. **(B) is the correct answer** because to the extent that price discrimination results in lower price and better availability of products, then society is benefitted. **(C) is incorrect** because the benefit sometimes is to consumers, especially consumers who might otherwise be priced out of the market. **(D) is incorrect** because price differences can be readily observed although in some situations price differences might occur through hidden rebates or other deals. But Choice (D) overstates the case about nonobservability of price discrimination.

185.   This question tests your knowledge of the defenses available under the Robinson-Patman Act. *See* United States v. Borden, 370 U.S. 460 (1962). **(A), (B), and (C) are each true, making them incorrect**. So **(D) is the correct answer**.

186.   This question tests your understanding of predatory pricing under the Robinson-Patman Act. A predatory pricing scheme through price discrimination operates much like a predatory pricing scheme discussed in Chapter Eight under attempted monopolization. The main difference is that the firm charges differential prices for the same product and attempts to use the higher price to make up for the lower price. *See Brooke Group*, cited in the answer to Question 182, where this theory was reviewed by the Supreme Court. **(A) and (C) are incorrect** because the standards are the same. **(D) is incorrect** because there is no

requirement of special antitrust injury. **(B) is the correct answer** because recoupment of the losses may be impossible or difficult to prove by the plaintiff.

187. This question tests your knowledge of the practice of base point pricing, a practice used to price discriminate. Under base point pricing, a seller uses different base line points to calculate shipping costs and thereby imposes different prices on different buyers. *See* Corn Products Ref. Co. v. FTC., 324 U.S. 726 (1945). **(A) and (D) are incorrect** because the practice is not per se illegal and may reflect costs. **(C) is incorrect** because the differences reflect costs to the seller, not buyer. **(B) is the correct answer** since such practices might be defensible if they represent differences in the costs of shipping.

188. This question tests your understanding of defenses to a claim of illegal price discrimination, namely when are two products or services identical. *See* FTC v. Borden, 383 U.S. 637 (1966) (dealing with different types of evaporated milk). **(A), (B), and (C) are incorrect.** They are not examples because the products or services at issue are different. **(D) is the correct answer** because effectively the discounts for the identical product differ across buyers.

189. This question tests your understanding of secondary line injury price discrimination. Do not confuse secondary line injury with second degree price discrimination. The first is a legal concept; the second, an economic one. Injury in secondary line cases are measured by harm to consumers, which can arise in cases involving first, second, or third degree price discrimination. *See* Morton Salt, cited in the answer to Question 183, and Brooke Group, cited in the answer to Question 182. **(B) is the correct answer** because it correctly discusses injury to consumers. **(A), (C), and (D) are incorrect** because they do not measure harms to consumers.

190. This question tests your understanding of the due recognition defense, which allows a firm to give discounts to retailers based on marketing efforts as long the as the recognition is available to everyone on equal terms. *See Morton Salt*, case cited in answer to Question 183, and Smith Wholesale Co. v. Phillip Morris, 477 F.3d 854 (6th Cir. 2007). **(A) is incorrect** because the issue is one of discrimination among customers, not predation. **(B) is the correct answer** because the due recognition constitutes a defense. **(C) is incorrect** because there is no per se violation. **(D) is incorrect** because there is price discrimination.

191. This question tests your understanding of the meeting the competition defense to a Robinson-Patman claim, which permits price discrimination if the pricing strategy was in response to competition. *See* FTC v. Sun Oil, 371 U.S. 505 (1962). **(A) is incorrect** because it ignores the defense of meeting the competition. **(B) is the correct answer** because it recognizes the defense of meeting the competition. **(C) is incorrect** because it vaguely and confusingly states a rule from predatory pricing, which is not applicable here. **(D) is incorrect** because it misstates the rule about meeting the competition.

192. This question tests your understanding of the policy behind the Robinson-Patman Act. See the answer to Question 182 above. **(A) is incorrect** because price discrimination does not always improve social welfare. **(B) is incorrect** because the Robinson-Patman Act states claims separate from Section One of the Sherman Act. **(C) is incorrect** because preventing predation was not the sole goal of the Act. **(D) is the correct answer** because it states correctly the background to the Act.

193. This question tests your understanding of the economics and business practice underlying price discrimination. **(A) is the correct answer** because if a firm cannot distinguish between customers, then it will not be able to charge different prices. Furthermore, if resale were possible, the resale market would put pressure on the market to keep prices down and make it more difficult to charge different prices. **(B) is incorrect** since competitors' costs are irrelevant to charging differential prices. **(C) is incorrect** because alternative sources of supply constitute irrelevant information. **(D) is incorrect** because this relationship is relevant to predation, not to differential pricing.

194. Price discrimination is charging a different price to different customers for the same product or service. An example would be charging a different price for students or senior citizens for a movie or giving discounts for bulk purchases of food. Antitrust law is concerned with price discrimination because in order to implement a price discrimination policy, a firm must have market power. Under antitrust laws, firms with market power can hurt market competition. Specifically, in the retail context, antitrust law was concerned with larger retail companies getting special price deals from wholesalers or manufacturers to the detriment of smaller companies. This practice of price discounts for larger retailers was the basis for the Robinson-Patman Act that covers price discrimination that had an adverse effect on competition.

195. Price discrimination can be understood by comparison to the practice of charging the same price to all consumers. Under this latter practice, consumers who cannot afford paying the price will not be able to purchase the product or service. The firm could serve these consumers by lowering its price. But if it charged the lower price for everyone, then the firm might not be able to make money. Price discrimination would allow the firm to serve more consumers. However, in order to price discriminate, the firm has to be able to sustain different prices. The firm can do this by preventing resale of the product or service. These controls of resale impose costs on the firm and on society. In addition, price discrimination requires a firm to have market power. The existence of market power might lead to anticompetitive effects as discussed in Question 194.

PRACTICE FINAL EXAM: ANSWERS

196. This question tests your understanding of horizontal restraints and price fixing. Please review the materials in Chapter Four as background to this question. **(A) is incorrect** because market power is not relevant for a Section One claim. **(B) is incorrect** because a monopsony is not exempt from the antitrust laws. **(C) is incorrect** because a joint venture in general is not subject to the rule of reason. **(D) is the correct answer** because the firms are engaged in horizontal price fixing.

197. This question tests your understanding of horizontal restraints and group boycotts. Please review the materials in Chapter Four as background to this question. **(A) is the correct answer** since the acts constitute a group boycott. **(B) is incorrect** because the statement about no duty to cooperate applies to Section Two claims. **(C) is incorrect** because if a violation of the Clayton Act, it would also violate the Sherman Act. **(D) is incorrect** because as a group boycott, it would be subject to per se analysis.

198. This question tests your understanding of horizontal restraints. Please review the materials in Chapter Four as background to this question. **(A) is the correct answer** since the agreement is among competitors in a market. **(B) is incorrect** because the agreement is horizontal. **(C) is incorrect** because there would be a question of whether the agreements fell into a per se category. **(D) is incorrect** because the agreements are horizontal, not vertical.

199. This question tests your understanding of monopolization claims and the relationship between Section One and Section Two claims. The question also involves joint ventures and the question of when there is unilateral conduct. Please review the materials in Chapters Six, Seven and Eight as background to this question. **(A) is incorrect** because there is no such category as predatory per se. **(B) is the correct answer** since it states the elements for a claim of predation. **(C) is incorrect** because in setting prices APA is acting as a single entity. **(D) is incorrect** because the agreement to form APA might be actionable under Section One.

200. This question tests your understanding of refusals to deal, or group boycotts, and the relationship between Section One and Section Two claims. Please review the materials in Chapters Four and Six as background to this question. **(A) is incorrect** because the independent firm has not engaged in monopolistic conduct. **(B) is incorrect** because the restraint at issue is not illegal. **(C) is the correct answer** since APA might be liable under Section Two and those agreed to form APA, liable under Section One. **(D) is incorrect** because antitrust law limits contracts that are anticompetitive.

201. This question tests your understanding of tying arrangements. Please review the materials in Chapters Five and Seven as background to this question. **(A), (B), and (D) are each accurate, and, therefore, incorrect. (C) is the correct answer** because the products are

separate ones and there must be two products or services for a tying claim.

202. This question tests your understanding of minimum resale price maintenance. Please review the material in Chapter Five as background to this question. **(A) is incorrect** because the customer is a direct purchaser. **(B) is incorrect** because the minimum price restraint is subject to rule of reason. **(C) is the correct answer** because minimum resale price maintenance is subject to the rule of reason. **(D) is incorrect** because market power is irrelevant to the treatment of minimum price restraints.

203. This question tests your understanding of the duty to cooperate under Section Two of the Sherman Act. Please review the materials in Chapter Seven as background to this question. **(A) is the correct answer** because there is no general duty to cooperate unless the facts fall within those of the Aspen Skiing case. **(B) is incorrect** because actual termination is not required if the parties have agreed as to price. **(C) is incorrect** because there is antitrust injury as a direct purchaser. **(D) is incorrect** because market power is irrelevant to the refusal to deal claim.

204. This question tests your understanding of horizontal restraints and refusals to deal. Please review the materials in Chapter Four as background to this question. **(A) is incorrect** because the price fixing is vertical subject to the rule of reason. **(B) is the correct answer** because the restraint at issue will be subject to the rule of reason. **(C)** and **(D) are incorrect** because the plaintiff has standing as a direct purchaser and there is antitrust injury.

205. This question tests your understanding of a technological tying arrangement similar to the one at issue in *Berkey Photo*. Please review the materials in Chapter Seven as background to this question. **(A) is incorrect** because there is no presumption of market power. **(B) is the correct answer** because a more efficient design can justify the technology. **(C) is incorrect** because having two products is only one of the requirements for a tying claim. **(D) is incorrect** because there is a strong argument that the products are distinct and do not constitute one product.

206. This question tests your understanding of the policies behind the antitrust laws. Please review the materials in Chapters One and Two as background to this question. **(A) is incorrect** because sometimes large firms can lead to innovation. **(B) is the correct answer** because it states the treatment of vertical restraints, as reflected in the Leegin decision. **(C) is incorrect** because economic theory would support large retail chains and some forms of price discrimination. **(D) is incorrect** because the big issue under economic theory is the possibility of recoupment.

207. This question tests your understanding of price discrimination. Please review the materials in Chapter Ten as background to this question. **(A) is incorrect** because price discrimination can maximize gains to consumers outside first degree price discrimination, as described in this answer choice. **(B) is the correct answer** because it illustrates second degree price discrimination. **(C) is incorrect** because allowing the good to be resold undermines price discrimination. **(D) is incorrect** because price discrimination is not per se illegal.

208. This question tests your understanding of the terminology and policies behind the antitrust laws. Please review the materials in Chapter One as background to this question. **(A), (B), and (C) are each accurate statements, and, therefore, incorrect. (D) is the correct**

answer because minimum resale price setting is subject to the rule of reason.

209. This question tests your understanding of the relationship between Section One and Section Two claims and the requirements of proof under Matsushita, Trinko and Twombly. Please review the materials in Chapters Four and Seven as background to this question. **(A) is incorrect** because the predation claim would also require a showing of the possibility of recoupment. **(B) is the correct answer** since under Twombly the claim of agreement has to be plausible and under Matsushita, the plaintiff has to show that recoupment is possible and predation in plausible. **(C) is incorrect** because the likelihood of an agreement has to be plausible to go past a motion to dismiss. **(D) is incorrect** because the issue of recoupment will be a basis to grant summary judgment to the defendant.

210. This question tests your understanding of mergers and the HHI. Please review the materials in Chapter Nine as background to this question. **(A) is the correct answer.** The HHI indicates a concentrated market and the increase implies that it will be more concentrated. **(B), (C), and (D) are incorrect** because they do not reflect this interpretation of the HHI.

211. This question tests your understanding of the economics of markets as applied to antitrust. Please review the materials in Chapter Two as background to this question. **(A) is incorrect** because the review is not more extensive for an oligopoly than for other markets. **(B) is incorrect** because barriers to entry are not necessarily low. **(C) is the correct answer** because the answer correctly defines an oligopoly and makes the point that collusion may be easier to sustain with fewer firms. **(D) is incorrect** because price competition might very likely exist in an oligopoly.

212. This question tests your understanding of antitrust procedure and the relationship with judicial process. Please review the materials in Chapter Three as background to this question. **(C) is the correct answer. (A), (B), and (D) are incorrect** because they do not take into account there is both an objective and a subjective element to the validity of the claim which determines whether an antitrust claim would survive.

213. This question tests your understanding of antitrust procedure and the relationship with administrative proceedings, under the Noerr-Pennington Doctrine. Please review the materials in Chapter Three as background to this question. **(A) is incorrect** because petitioning is protected under the Noerr-Pennington Doctrine. **(B) is incorrect** because there is no absolute immunity. **(C) is the correct answer** because it correctly describes the Noerr-Pennington Doctrine. **(D) is incorrect**, but close. Active supervision is a basis for municipal immunity under the antitrust laws, but in this case the question is asking about the person bringing the petition.

214. This question tests your understanding of the relationship between antitrust and other economic or industry regulation. Please review the materials in Chapter Three as background to this question. **(A), (C), and (D) are accurate, making them incorrect. (B) is the correct answer** because it inaccurately states the treatment of antitrust claims in the telecommunications industry. Antitrust claims in deregulated industries have been more difficult to bring because the new regulatory environment often entails new market structures created by Congress.

215. This question tests your understanding about antitrust law's relationship to intellectual property law. Please review the materials in Chapters Three and Seven as background to this question. **(A), (C), and (D) are accurate, making them incorrect. (B) is the correct answer** because there is no presumption of market power that stems from patent ownership.

216. This question tests your understanding of identifying different types of business practices and their treatment under the antitrust laws. Please review the materials in Chapters Four and Six as background to this question. **(D) is the correct answer** since the agreement is among competitors in a market. **(A) is incorrect** because the agreement is among competitors. **(B) is incorrect** because we do not know about market power and how many other firms might still be in the market. **(C) is incorrect** because the Program is one entity and so does not fit the case of oligopoly.

217. This question tests your understanding of different types of business practices and their treatment under the antitrust laws. Please review the materials in Chapter Seven as background to this question. **(A) is incorrect** because the agreement to form the Program is among several entities, creating the basis for a Section One claim. **(B) is the correct answer** because the Program is one entity acting unilaterally. However, the agreement to form the Program could be subject to a Section One claim. **(C) is incorrect** because there does not appear to be any restraints placed on employers that would subject the agreement to antitrust scrutiny. **(D) is incorrect** because such leveraging is possible but is a per se violation only if there is market power.

218. This question tests your understanding of horizontal restraints. Please review the materials in Chapters One and Four as background to this question. **(B) is the correct answer** because the principal agreement is about the salary and the retention is subsidiary. Since the agreement about salary, which is a type of price, it is a price fixing agreement. The retention term is an ancillary restraint. **(A), (C), and (D) are incorrect** because they state variations on the correct treatment of the two claims.

219. This question tests your understanding of antitrust procedure and the Noerr-Pennington Doctrine. Please review the materials in Chapter Three as background to this question. **(A) is incorrect** because Noerr-Pennington applies to lobbying and other exercise of political or legal processes. Such an exercise is not at issue here. **(B) is the correct answer** since the law schools are not petitioning a government body like a legislature or a zoning board. **(C) is incorrect** because efficiencies are not relevant to the immunity. **(D) is incorrect** because it vaguely states a rule applicable to antitrust claims based on sham litigation.

220. This question tests your understanding of a refusal to deal, also called a group boycott. Please review the materials in Chapter Four as background to this question. **(A) is incorrect** because the refusal to deal is not ancillary. It is part of the agreement. **(B) is incorrect** because this is an agreement among competitors and therefore horizontal. **(C) is the correct answer** under the Klor's decision, cited in Question 64. **(D) is incorrect** because this is not an exclusive dealership but an example of group boycott.

221. This question reviews the points from Questions 99 and 100. Vertical agreements have competitive benefits that might outweigh potential anticompetitive effects. The anticompetitive effects of horizontal agreements may in some situations outweigh

competitive benefits, such as with price fixing or territorial divisions. Therefore, pe se rules are appropriate for some horizontal agreements with rule of reason being appropriate for vertical agreements.

222.   A monopoly is a market with one firm. Although antitrust law is primarily concerned with preserving competition, a monopoly might be the product of a successful competitor who has had good luck, strong business acumen, or a provider of an innovative product or service. Despite its commitment to competition, antitrust law does not want to punish luck or business acumen. Furthermore, a monopolist might be subject to competition through the entry of a new firm that might have even better products that can benefit consumers. Therefore, antitrust law is concerned if a monopoly tries to prevent competitive entry through exclusionary or predatory conduct. Furthermore, antitrust law is concerned if a monopoly tries to expand its market power through leveraging.

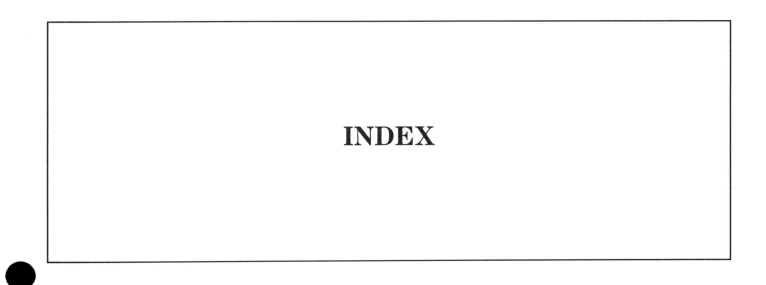

INDEX

INDEX